HEALTH CARE ISSUES, COSTS AND ACCESS

LONG-TERM CARE

CONSIDERATIONS AND FEDERAL RECOMMENDATIONS FOR LONG-TERM SERVICES AND SUPPORTS

HEALTH CARE ISSUES, COSTS AND ACCESS

Additional books in this series can be found on Nova's website under the Series tab.

Additional E-books in this series can be found on Nova's website under the E-book tab.

HEALTH CARE ISSUES, COSTS AND ACCESS

LONG-TERM CARE

CONSIDERATIONS AND FEDERAL RECOMMENDATIONS FOR LONG-TERM SERVICES AND SUPPORTS

KEVIN PICKENS
EDITOR

nova publishers
New York

For permission to use material from this book please contact us:
Telephone 631-231-7269; Fax 631-231-8175
Web Site: http://www.novapublishers.com

Additional color graphics may be available in the e-book version of this book.

Library of Congress Cataloging-in-Publication Data

ISBN: 978-1-63117-108-6

Published by Nova Science Publishers, Inc. † New York

CONTENTS

Preface		**vii**
Chapter 1	Report to the Congress of the Commission on Long Term Care	**1**
Chapter 2	Factors Affecting the Demand for Long-Term Care Insurance: Issues for Congress *Janemarie Mulvey*	**125**
Index		**153**

PREFACE

Over 12 million Americans of all ages with functional impairments today rely on personal assistance and other long-term services and supports (LTSS) in their home and community or in an institution to perform daily activities to maintain their quality of living and, when possible, their independence. Most of them receive services and supports from dedicated caregivers that enable them to cope with their cognitive or physical limitations with dignity. This book provides a report to the Congress of the Commission on long term care and discusses issues for congress on the factors affecting the demand for long term care insurance.

Chapter 1 – The Commission on Long-Term Care was established under Section 643 of American Taxpayer Relief Act of 2012 (P.L. 112–240), signed into law January 2, 2013. The Commission was established with 15 members. Three members each were appointed by the President of the United States, the majority leader of the Senate, the minority leader of the Senate, the Speaker of the House of Representatives, and the minority leader of the House of Representatives. The Commission elected Dr. Bruce Chernof as its Chair and Dr. Mark Warshawsky as its Vice-Chair.

The statute directed the Commission to: "...develop a plan for the establishment, implementation, and financing of a comprehensive, coordinated, and high-quality system that ensures the availability of long-term services and supports for individuals in need of such services and supports, including elderly individuals, individuals with substantial cognitive or functional limitations, other individuals who require assistance to perform activities of daily living, and individuals desiring to plan for future long-term care needs."

Chapter 2 – As the 80 million baby boomers approach retirement, many are concerned they will not have sufficient savings to sustain their standard of living in retirement. Few, however, may be focused on another risk to their retirement security—the potential cost of financing often expensive longterm care services and supports (LTSS). LTSS include help with either functional or cognitive impairment and generally include assistance with activities such as bathing, eating, and dressing. For the majority of older Americans, the cost of obtaining paid help for these services may far exceed their financial resources in the future. Private long-term care insurance (LTCI) is available to provide some financial protection for persons against the risk of the potentially high cost of LTSS. In 2010, about 6% of LTSS spending was paid by LTCI. This low rate of financing reflects relatively low demand for LTCI over the past few decades. Moreover, most policy owners have not yet reached the age where they may need services. In 2010, between 7 million to 9 million Americans owned a private LTCI policy, with about 11% of the population aged 55 and older covered by a policy. A number of factors have adversely affected the demand for LTCI. The cost and complexity of LTCI policies have been cited as major deterrents to purchasing LTCI. In addition, increased concerns have arisen about the adequacy of consumer protections for LTCI as a result of inconsistencies in LTCI laws and regulations across the states. More recently, adverse publicity about premium increases and heightened concerns about the future solvency of LTCI insurers in the current economic environment have further dampened demand, prompting state regulators to re-evaluate current regulations and laws governing LTCI. The private LTCI market has undergone significant changes in the past three decades. The employer-sponsored market has grown as a share of total LTCI sales and the overall market has become more concentrated in terms of the number of companies selling the product. A number of newer product lines have been introduced that combine LTCI with other products, such as retirement annuities and life-insurance products. To address these issues, the 113th Congress may consider a number of legislative options to increase participation in the voluntary LTCI market. These may include proposals to increase tax incentives to lower the after-tax cost of policies, improve consumer protections to boost consumer confidence in the product, and expand consumer education. This report discusses the role of LTCI in financing LTSS and current trends in the LTCI industry; factors affecting the demand for LTCI, including cost and complexity of the product and adequacy of consumer protections; and legislative options available to address these issues.

In: Long-Term Care
Editor: Kevin Pickens

ISBN: 978-1-63117-108-6

Chapter 1

REPORT TO THE CONGRESS OF THE COMMISSION ON LONG TERM CARE*

INTRODUCTION

The Commission on Long-Term Care was established under Section 643 of American Taxpayer Relief Act of 2012 (P.L. 112–240), signed into law January 2, 2013. The Commission was established with 15 members. Three members each were appointed by the President of the United States, the majority leader of the Senate, the minority leader of the Senate, the Speaker of the House of Representatives, and the minority leader of the House of Representatives. The Commission elected Dr. Bruce Chernof as its Chair and Dr. Mark Warshawsky as its Vice-Chair.

The statute directed the Commission to: "...develop a plan for the establishment, implementation, and financing of a comprehensive, coordinated, and high-quality system that ensures the availability of long-term services and supports for individuals in need of such services and supports, including elderly individuals, individuals with substantial cognitive or functional limitations, other individuals who require assistance to perform activities of daily living, and individuals desiring to plan for future long-term care needs."

The statute further directed the Commission within 6 months of the appointment of Commissioners (by September 12, 2013) to: "…vote on a comprehensive and detailed report based on the long-term care plan…

* This is an edited, reformatted and augmented version of the Commission on Long Term Care publication, dated September 30, 2013.

[described above]… that contains any recommendations or proposals for legislative or administrative action as the Commission deems appropriate, including proposed legislative language to carry out the recommendations or proposals."

The Commission convened its first meeting on June 27, 2013. It held four public hearings with testimony for 34 witnesses. It solicited extensive comments from the general public. It met in 9 executive sessions. The Commission met on September 12, 2013 and voted, by a vote of 9 to 6, in favor of putting this Final Report forward as the broad agreement of the Commission.

On the question: "Should the report be put forward as the broad agreement of the Commission?" the vote was:

- Yeas: Chernof, Warshawsky, Anwar, Brachman, Guillard, Pruitt, Raphael, Turner, and Vradenburg
- Nays: Butler, Claypool, Feder, Jacobs, Ruttledge, and Stein

SECTION I. A CALL TO ACTION

Over 12 million Americans of all ages with functional impairments today rely on personal assistance and other long-term services and supports (LTSS) in their home and community or in an institution to perform daily activities to maintain their quality of living and, when possible, their independence. Most of them receive services and supports from dedicated caregivers that enable them to cope with their cognitive or physical limitations with dignity. The services and supports they receive are provided by family or friends who provide unpaid assistance out of love and commitment and by paid caregivers who have chosen to earn their living in an intensely personal caring profession.

LTSS are essential but costly for individuals with cognitive and functional limitations and their families. Family caregivers sacrifice other family and work responsibilities and bear a financial and emotional burden that can be overwhelming. Paid services and supports are expensive, and when received over an extended period of time, can be financially catastrophic. Individuals and families rarely have sufficient resources (either savings or private insurance) to pay for an extended period of LTSS. Medicaid provides a critical safety net for those with few resources or who have exhausted nearly all of their resources paying for care. Nearly two-thirds of the cost of LTSS today is financed by the federal and state governments through the Medicaid program.

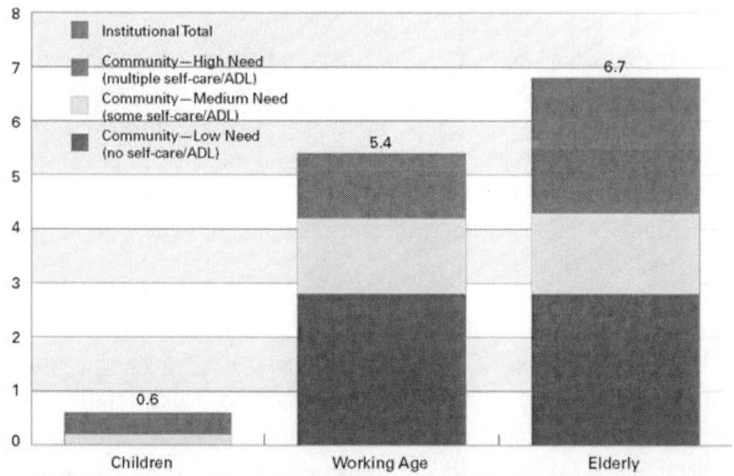

Source: S. Kaye, data from 2012 NHIS, 2010 Census, Nursing Home Data Compendium 2010.

Population Needing LTSS, by Age Group and Level of Need (Millions).

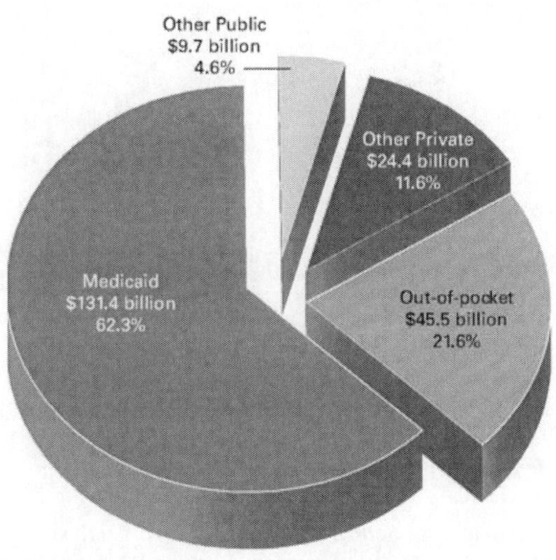

Source: National Health Policy Forum, based on data from 2011 National Health Expenditure Accounts.

LTSS Expenditures by Source, 2011.

LTSS have improved substantially in recent decades. Yet problems remain for individuals and families who need care, notwithstanding the commitment and dedication of thousands of paid and family caregivers providing loving and quality services. Paid services and supports are highly fragmented and difficult for individuals and family caregivers to access, lacking the focus and coordination across agencies and providers necessary to ensure the best outcomes for the person and family, and are provided in ways that can be expensive and inefficient. The need for LTSS and the costs of paid LTSS must be addressed in the context of the financial pressures for many American families and the fiscal challenges, including population aging and high health care costs, which face our Nation.

A dramatic projected increase in the need for LTSS in coming decades will confront significant constraints in the resources available to provide LTSS. Aging Baby Boomers will grow the numbers of older Americans with physical and cognitive limitations. At the same time, fewer family caregivers combined with more limited personal financial resources to pay for caregiving due to declines in savings rates, retirement asset accumulation, and private insurance purchase, will place increasing pressure on the Medicaid program and the federal and state budgets that fund it. Governments will have to balance growing LTSS needs with education, public health and safety, and other priorities.

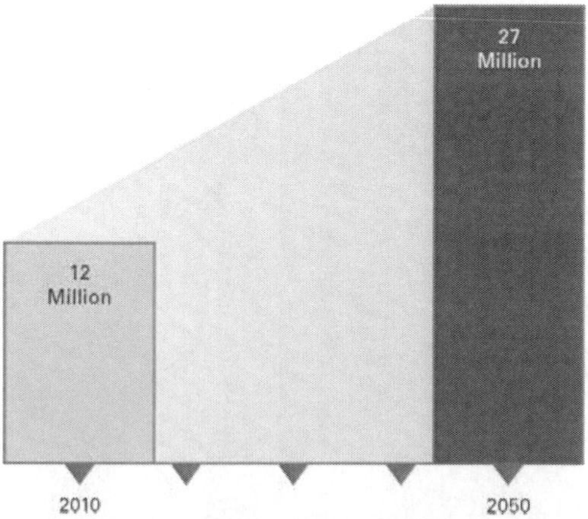

Source: S. Kaye, C. Harrington, and M. Laplante (2010). Analysis of 2005 SIPP, 2007 NHIS, 2007 ACS, 2004 NHHS, and the 2005–2006 Medical Expenditure Survey.

The Number of Americans Needing Long-Term Care Will More than Double by 2050.

New approaches are needed to bring LTSS care integration, technology, and innovative workforce strategies together to reduce the overall cost of achieving better health and well-being outcomes for individuals and their families. Many persons living with disabilities are able and want to participate in the workforce. Changes are needed to support them so they can receive the LTSS they need for full workforce participation. Creative financing efforts are needed to affordably insure the risk of needing LTSS and encourage higher levels of savings. Finally, a more accessible and sustainable Medicaid is needed to assure its continued role in guaranteeing the availability of LTSS for individuals and families with few resources to provide for themselves.

Now is the time to put these new approaches and efforts in place if the coming generations of Americans are to have access to the array of LTSS needed to remain independent themselves or to assure the safety and well-being of a loved one with substantial physical or cognitive limitations. The need is great. The time to act is now.

Section II. Specific Challenges to Providing LTSS

Over 12 million Americans and their families are confronted with long-term functional and cognitive limitations and face the challenge of arranging and financing or providing the necessary assistance with performing daily activities. This Section defines long-term services and supports (LTSS) and describes specific structure and process challenges experienced by American families in three key domains – service delivery, workforce, and financing.

What are Long-Term Services and Supports?

- Long-term services and supports (LTSS) are defined as assistance with activities of daily living (ADLs, including bathing, dressing, eating, transferring, walking[1]) and instrumental activities of daily living (IADLs, including meal preparation, money management, house cleaning, medication management, transportation[2]) to people who cannot perform these activities on their own due to a physical, cognitive, developmental, or chronic health condition that is expected to continue for an extended period of time, typically 90 days or more.
- LTSS include such things as human assistance, supervision, cueing and stand-by assistance, assistive technologies, workplace supports,

and care and service coordination for people who live in their own homes, community residential settings, or institutional settings.

- LTSS are a distinct set of services from health care services, although they may include health-related services. LTSS are a critical element of support and service for persons who are receiving health care services for severe chronic health conditions or disabilities that contribute to their functional limitations.
- LTSS include both paid assistance and assistance provided by family members and other unpaid caregivers.[3]

Who Has Functional Limitations?

- The 12 million Americans who rely on LTSS are a diverse group in terms of age, the condition causing functional incapacity, and place of residence. People who rely on LTSS are almost equally split between adults who are age 65 and older (56 percent) and adults under 65 (44 percent). Adults are 96 percent of the total population who rely on LTSS.[4]
- Responding to LTSS needs is often contingent on an individual's stage of life and circumstances.
    - Children under the age of 18 are a small percentage of the total population requiring LTSS, but can have substantial needs that will last a lifetime. For the most part, their care is provided by their families. Their functional limitations primarily result from impairments that occur at birth or infancy. Their impairments are equally split between physical and intellectual/ developmental disabilities (I/DD) with a significant number experiencing mental health disorders.[5]
    - The top ranking conditions for working-age adults with functional limitations between the ages of 18 and 44 who need LTSS include intellectual disabilities, paralysis and nervous system disorders, back problems and mental health disorders.
    - The majority of those needing LTSS in the 45 to 64 age group have adult onset disabilities, primarily consisting of physical disabilities with a significant number of those also suffering from mental health disabilities.
    - About half of the physical functional impairments associated with LTSS needs of older adults have onset after age 65 (90 percent

after age 18) and are caused primarily by arthritis, heart condition and diabetes. Dementia and stroke, however, are both major causes of impairment, especially for the 22 percent of older adults needing LTSS who do not have physical impairments. Cognitive impairment is a complicating comorbidity for many other LTSS users.[6] Alzheimer's disease, the most common form of dementia, accounting for 60–80 percent of dementia cases, almost always results in a need for LTSS.[7] One in 8 Americans over the age of 65 has Alzheimer's, and the disease affects 42.5 percent of Americans over the age 85.[8]

- These different populations have different needs that can be met with similar services and supports, but are often provided in different settings or care systems. For the older population, ability to work is not a factor in eligibility for assistance. For working-age persons with functional limitations, eligibility for income support and related health benefits is typically based on the inability to work.[9] The need for LTSS, however, is related to functional impairment, which may exist in a context in which the individual is unable to work or in which assistance is needed to maintain employment. Many adults with functional limitations are able to work with personal assistance, workplace supports, and other LTSS.

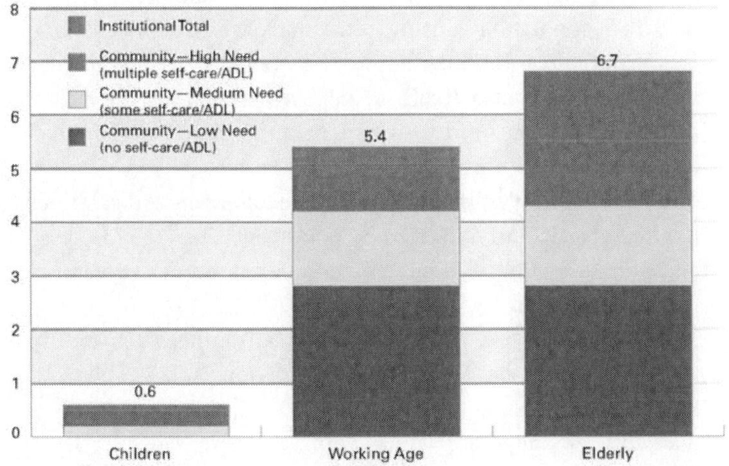

Source: S. Kaye, data from 2012 NHIS, 2010 Census, Nursing Home Data Compendium 2010.

Population Needing LTSS, by Age Group and Level of Need (Millions).

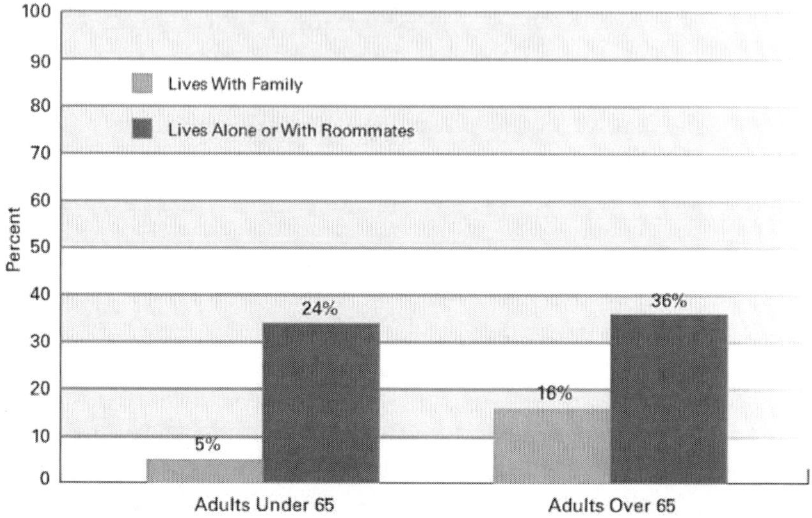

Source: S. Kaye, analysis of 2010 SIPP data.

Use of Paid Help Among Community-Resident Adults Needing LTSS.

- The shift of the population receiving paid LTSS from institutional to home and community-based care ("de-institutionalization") has had the greatest impact on care for the under 65 population in need of LTSS. Among Medicaid beneficiaries, nearly 80 percent of the under-65 LTSS population is using community-based services, compared to less than half of the older adult LTSS population.[10] Non-elderly adult LTSS users are also likely to depend entirely on their families for care—less than a third use paid help compared to over half of the older adult LTSS users.[11]
- The population with intellectual and developmental disabilities (I/DD) has been particularly affected by policy decisions to close large public and private institutions and shift to community-based care, in part in response to litigation.[12]
- There are racial and ethnic disparities in the need for and the use of LTSS. Older black and Hispanic individuals have higher rates of functional impairment than whites.[13] Nursing home use has declined markedly among older whites, but has increased over time among older blacks and now exceeds the usage rate among whites.[14] Growth in nursing home use has been especially rapid among older Hispanics and Asians in recent years, albeit from a very low rate.[15] Researchers

have found many reasons for racial and ethnic disparities, including stronger reliance on or preference for family-provided informal care, disparities in area resources, and differences in economic status.[16] Black residents remain more likely to live in nursing homes that have deficiencies in care.[17]

- The number of people needing LTSS is expected to grow in the next few decades as the Baby-Boom generation ages, although trends in age-adjusted rates of disability now appear to be holding steady after a period of improvement for older populations.[18] The number of individuals with Alzheimer's and other dementias will increase as the number of elderly people increases. By 2050, the annual number of new cases of Alzheimer's is projected to more than double.[19]

The Critical Role of Family Caregiving

- Most people who receive LTSS in the home rely on family caregiving. A "family caregiver" may be a relative, partner, friend, or neighbor who has a significant relationship with, and provides assistance for, a person who has functional limitations.
- Family caregivers are a major part of the care delivery system, providing the majority of LTSS and often coordinating paid LTSS and health care. Many caregivers also contribute direct financial support to individuals with daily functional needs to remain in their homes and remain as independent as possible. On a typical day in 2009, 42 million family caregivers nationwide were providing care to an adult with LTSS needs, with women being the vast majority of unpaid caregivers.[20]
- The value of family caregiving exceeds the total value of all paid LTSS. Family caregiving was estimated to be worth $450 billion in 2009 [21] as compared to $211 billion in spending on all paid caregiving in 2011.[22] In addition, the cost to U.S. businesses from lost productivity from family caregiver employees (from reduced hours, replacement of employees, absenteeism, and other factors) was estimated at $34 billion dollars in 2004.[23]
- Families typically expect to and prefer to care for a loved one with a chronic illness or disability. In surveys, most Americans say they would feel obligated to care for a parent who needed assistance.[24] However, many family caregivers have no alternative to providing

care themselves due to the expense of paid care. Families with children in need of LTSS typically prefer to care for their children, but are likely to need support with complex care needs. Adults under age 65 with functional impairments are more likely to rely exclusively on family caregiving than older adults.[25]

- Caregiving often places financial, physical, and emotional hardship on the caregivers. Frequently caregivers have little advance knowledge or training in the activities they have to perform, have little access to information and support they need to help navigate the fragmented health and LTSS systems, and have no opportunity to arrange other support when they are unable to provide care.[26]
- Caring for an individual with cognitive limitations can pose a particular challenge. Approximately 15.4 million people provide care to individuals with Alzheimer's and other dementias. Caregivers of individuals with Alzheimer's and other dementias spend more years caregiving on average than family caregivers providing care to individuals without dementia, and are also more likely to report assisting their loved ones with at least one ADL, compared with caregivers of older adults in general. Moreover, caregivers of individuals with Alzheimer's report high levels of physical and emotional stress due to caregiving, and are more likely to suffer from depression than caregivers of older adults in general.[27]
- The nature of family caregiving is changing as more individuals are discharged early from acute settings with increasingly complex medical care needs to be met in the home. The increasing complexity of post-acute care is making care more challenging for family caregivers who are capably providing LTSS for a loved one, but often do not have training in the medical/nursing tasks they need to perform in the wake of an acute care episode.[28]
- While families will likely continue to be the primary support for individuals with LTSS needs, declining birth rates over the last 50 years mean there will be fewer family members available in the near future to provide hands-on support compared to the number of Baby Boomers who are providing care for an aging relative today. A recent AARP study projected a dramatic decline over the next 20 years in the caregiver support ratio: from 7 potential caregivers for every person in the high-risk years of 80-plus in 2010 to 4 for every person 80-plus in 2030.[29]

- The challenges family caregivers face, in the context of a likely decline in the future in the availability of family caregivers, threaten to increase the use of paid care, the burden on private financial resources, and the stress on publicly financed programs.

How Paid LTSS is Provided—Delivery System Challenges

- Individuals with substantial functional and cognitive needs struggle to participate in everyday activities of living, live safely and well at home or in their residence of choice, and to enjoy many aspects of daily life. Various services, ranging from personal care assistance, adaptive technologies, environmental modifications, and residential communities exist to address these difficulties.[30]
- However, the network of providers to deliver this support is complex, multi-faceted, specialized, isolated from other service providers, and confusing to the average consumer. Few providers in this network evaluate a person's overall situation in order to arrange for the right combination of services based on one's actual needs. Instead, access to services is often organized in relationship to their funding streams, governed by a mix of federal, state, and local rules and procedures. Separate agencies may have unique eligibility rules, intake and assessment processes.
- When the need for LTSS arises in the wake of a medical event—a hospitalization for an accident or illness, or a transition from a post-acute stay to longterm care—the planning and organization of LTSS for an individual is often handled separately from the health care planning, and there are few incentives for health care providers to integrate LTSS with medical care planning or service delivery. Patients may be discharged to a nursing home or their own home for post-acute care. When individuals need LTSS, frequently they and their families must find and arrange for LTSS on their own, sometimes on short notice when the need arises from a medical event or a change in the individual's functional capacity. Families responding on short notice rarely have the opportunity to make solid LTSS arrangements that will enable a safe living environment. When a fragile care system fails, individuals may experience a longer-than-needed hospital stay, an interim discharge to a nursing facility, and/or an unwarranted re-hospitalization.

- When people have to arrange paid LTSS, the fragmented system is difficult for the individual and family caregiver to access and negotiate. Currently, there is no comprehensive approach to care coordination for these individuals and caregivers. As a result, services and supports may not be provided in the most appropriate setting by the most appropriate provider, the individual's needs and preferences may not be met, and their caregivers may experience substantial stress trying to arrange for or provide care. This fragmented, provider and setting-centered approach (as opposed to a person-centered approach) results in service and supports needs that go unmet, putting individuals at risk for injuries and/or adverse health consequences requiring medical attention.
- Persons with functional limitations do not always have a choice of the LTSS they need in the least restrictive environment appropriate for their level of functioning.[31] The 1999 Supreme Court decision in *Olmstead* [32] required states to make reasonable accommodation to enable persons with disabilities to receive services in the most integrated setting appropriate to their needs. Since then, federal and state spending has shifted from primarily supporting institutional care to a more balanced mix of institutional and non-institutional care. Several initiatives have been funded aimed at increasing access for individuals with functional limitations to a choice of LTSS that can provide assistance with daily living toward the goal of maintaining their independence, self-determination, and dignity.
- The *Olmstead* decision resulted in substantial Medicaid funding and state waiver authority to increase access to home and community-based services (HCBS). Medicaid spending for HCBS has increased substantially both in amount and as a proportion of all Medicaid LTSS spending since 1997. The Bush Administration's New Freedom Initiative in 2001 and the Obama Administration's Community Living Initiative in 2009 included implementation of Aging and Disability Resource Centers (ADRCs) as a way to meet the intent of *Olmstead*. The ADRCs are intended to serve as single points of entry into the LTSS system for older adults, people with disabilities, families and others, to make efficient use of care options and maximize available services.

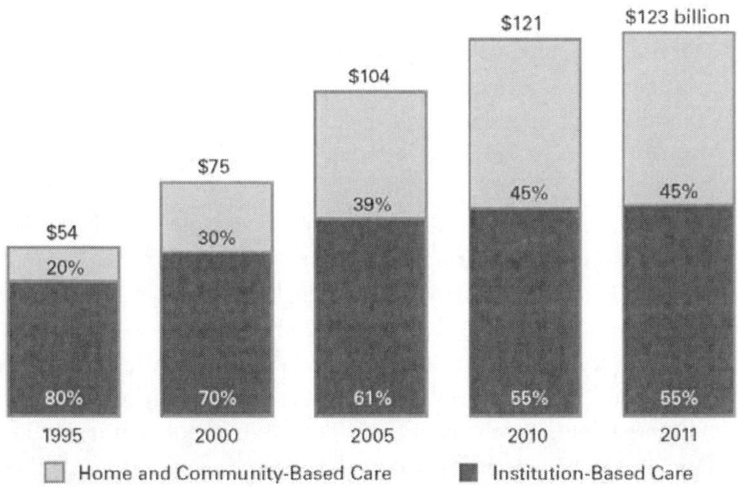

Source: Kaiser Commission on Medicaid and the Uninsured and Urban Institute analysis of CMS-64 data.

Medicaid Spending on Long-Term Care Has Been Shifting Toward Community-Based Care.

- However, results are inconsistent across the country, with state-by-state variations in eligibility and services provided through public sources and severe constraints on the availability of services in some states. There are significant access limits on many LTSS. Many states cap enrollment in HCBS, and some maintain waiting lists. An estimated 500,000 people are currently on state HCBS waiting lists of one kind or another.[33] Publicly-funded programs do not cover many services that are needed to remain independent (e.g., technology, home modifications, family supports). In addition, public funding is available to provide services and supports for people with disabilities who are not able to work but is not generally available to support persons with functional limitations who can and will work with assistance.
- There are a number of promising initiatives aimed at integrating LTSS with acute and post-acute care to develop a continuum of care that is person-and family-centered rather than centered on the setting or funding source. New organization and payment initiatives have the potential to align financial incentives of health care organizations to focus on and take accountability for health outcomes. Several states are pioneering comprehensive LTSS initiatives to combine

assessment, information, counseling, care management, and other services to empower persons with functional limitations to choose settings and services that best meet their needs. Most of these initiatives are pilot and small scale projects, reaching only a small part of the range of services and supports, consumers, and geographic areas in the U.S.

- The Program of All-inclusive Care for the Elderly (PACE), a well-known forerunner of many of today's community-based models of integrated care for dual beneficiaries, is an excellent case in point with respect to the challenges involved in bringing successful programs to scale. Initiated in 1990, PACE now serves over 25,000 enrollees nationally. A single model of financing and organizing care cannot serve the entire population in need. As of 1999, there were approximately 3 million elderly in the United States who met the eligibility criteria for PACE: community-based, nursing home-certifiable, and dually eligible, who could benefit from PACE or other integrated service options.[34]
- The Centers for Medicare and Medicaid Services (CMS) Medicare-Medicaid Coordination Office Financial Alignment Demonstration will test capitated and managed fee-for-service models on a large-scale basis for dually-eligible beneficiaries in which primary, acute and behavioral health services are covered in addition to LTSS. Eight states (Massachusetts, Washington, Ohio, Illinois, California, New York, Virginia, and Minnesota (through an alternative model)) were recently selected to begin full implementation of their demonstrations.[35]
- Several States, including Minnesota and Washington, are pioneering the development of innovative, 'high-functioning' LTSS systems which bring together easy-to-access information, assessment, counseling, care management, nursing home pre-admission and transition services and a wide array of home and community-based and managed care options.[36]
- Participant-directed or consumer-directed services are increasingly being offered under Medicaid home care waivers.[37] Under these programs, older adults and persons with a disability are approved for a certain number of hours according to their needs. They are then able to recruit, hire, and train their own personal care attendants to provide services; programs may also offer an agency option; and, in many states, family members may

take these jobs. Personal direction has proved very popular with care recipients, who feel more in control of their care.[38] To facilitate the individual employment of direct care workers, Medicaid programs set up fiscal intermediaries to process paychecks and file payroll taxes.[39]

Who Provides Paid LTSS?: Workforce Challenges

- The workforce providing paid LTSS is a critical link in the availability and quality of services. It is a mix of professionals and direct care workers who are found in a number of settings, such as nursing homes, institutions for individuals with intellectual and developmental disabilities, and in home and community-based settings.
- The professional workforce includes physicians, nursing home and assisted living administrators, registered nurses (RNs), licensed practical and vocational nurses (LVN/LPNs),[40] physical and occupational therapists, and social workers.[41] However, nurses provide the majority of professional long-term care. RNs tend to hold supervisory roles in nursing homes and home health agencies, while LPNs provide direct patient care, including tasks such as medication administration and taking vital signs.[42]
- Direct care workers include nursing aides and orderlies, home health aides, and personal care and home care aides. Nursing aides and orderlies work primarily in nursing homes and assisted living facilities, and perform both paramedical tasks and assistance with ADLs. Home health aides perform tasks similar to those of nursing aides, but in the home and community. Personal care attendants, also called personal care aides and home care workers, generally provide social supports and assistance with ADLS to individuals in their homes.[43]
- The professional workforce specifically trained to meet the LTSS needs of the older adult population will not be adequate to meet the future needs for LTSS. There were only 7,356 board-certified geriatricians in the United States in 2012,[44] and there is only about one geriatric psychiatrist for every 23,000 older adults. By 2030, this will fall to one for every 43,000 older adults.[45] In addition, less than 4 percent of social workers specialize in aging, despite the fact that 75

percent report working with older adults.[46] Nurses, who provide a significant amount of care for older adults, have high rates of turnover in nursing homes.[47]

- The direct care workforce provides between 70 and 80 percent of paid long-term personal assistance.[48] Due to the aging of the population and the rebalancing towards home and community-based services, demand for direct care workers is set to increase by 48 percent over the next decade, adding 1.6 million positions.[49] The anticipated increase in the demand for workers could lead to a shortage of experienced workers.[50] Retention is also an issue. While some workers have stable job tenure, others have low job and industry attachment. Studies of turnover have found rates of 44–46 percent for home care workers, 49 percent for certified nurse assistants (CNAs) in nursing homes, and 26 percent among CNAs in assisted living facilities.[51] CNAs have a 49 percent retention rate in nursing homes, and a 78 percent retention rate in assisted living facilities. Agencies have reported difficulty attracting and retaining qualified workers,[52] which may affect the quality of care that individuals with LTSS needs receive.

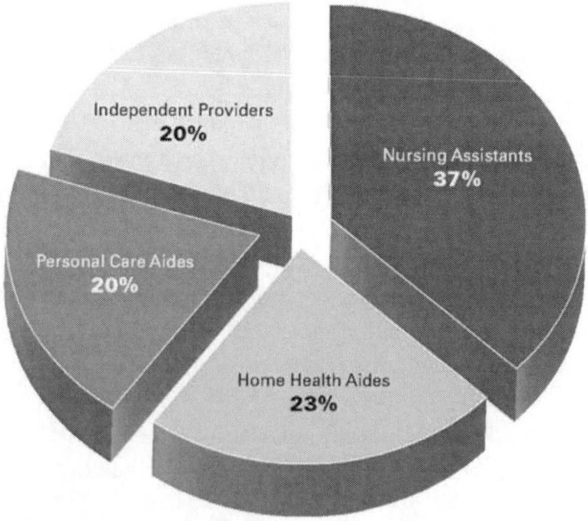

Source: PHI analysis of BLS 2012 data.

Direct Care Workforce, 2012.

- Factors that contribute to the difficulty in attracting and retaining experienced direct care workers are the low levels of compensation, lack of benefits, and limited opportunities for advancement that are associated with the skill levels required for the job.[53] In addition, compensation has not increased for these jobs over the last decade.[54] Compensation is generally higher for direct care workers in nursing homes than in home and community-based settings. However, nursing home positions also exhibit high turnover, due not only to low compensation, but also to high caseloads and supervisory style. For example, nursing aides are more likely to stay with their positions if they feel valued and respected.[55] Demographic changes will also affect the supply of direct care workers. The growth of the labor pool of women aged 25 to 54, from which direct care workers are primarily drawn, is not expected to keep pace with the demand for workers.[56]
- With the increase in HCBS, it is likely that workers will tend to serve consumers with more complex needs with less supervision. At the same time, nursing home residents are projected to become increasingly elderly and frail.[57] Experts are concerned that direct care workers serving consumers with increasingly complex care needs do not receive adequate training.[58] At the federal level, there is currently no minimum training requirement for personal care attendants. Home Health Aides and CNAs who work at Medicare-certified agencies are both required to have 75 hours of training, of which 16 must be clinically supervised. In 2008, the Institute of Medicine recommended raising this requirement to at least 120 hours of training, but most states have not adopted this standard.[59] The training requirements for consumer-directed personal care aides are even more minimal.[60] In addition to leaving workers unprepared for the tasks they might face at work, lack of training or career pathways also makes it difficult for workers to advance.[61] Training has also been shown to reduce turnover and increase job satisfaction among direct care workers.[62]
- High turnover and workforce shortages have an impact on care quality. Though there is little data about the effect of worker turnover in home and community-based settings, studies in nursing homes have shown that higher turnover is associated with poor quality of care as measured by use of restraints, pressure ulcers, psychoactive drug use, and certification survey quality of care deficiencies.[63]

Paying for LTSS: Financing Challenges

- Paid LTSS are labor-intensive and can be costly due to the duration of care.[64] Traditionally, LTSS has been the responsibility of family caregivers. But when paid services are needed, most Americans are not effectively prepared to shoulder the cost, whether services are needed due to a disability with onset at birth, during working years, or in old age.
- Individual needs for LTSS for those under the age of 65 vary widely due to the diverse nature of the conditions being addressed. Individuals with a permanent condition may face LTSS costs that have a long duration that can be costly. Children and pre-65 adults and their families are unlikely to have access to long-term care insurance, due to their condition and the limitations of insurance that would cover these expenses, and are unlikely to have accumulated substantial assets. A high percentage of them will rely on Medicaid to finance care when they need paid care. The population with functional impairments due to intellectual and developmental disabilities are most dependent on Medicaid funding—77 percent of the funding for I/DD services and supports comes from the Medicaid program,[65] compared to 61 percent of the LTSS funding for the total non-elderly adult population and 22 percent of the LTSS funding for the elderly population.[66]
- Working-age adults with disabilities who continue to work have extra expenses associated with disability such as personal assistance, mobility devices, and assistive technology, among others. These supports are necessary for employment but require more resources to achieve the same outcomes as their nondisabled counterparts. Medicaid is the only program that provides LTSS for individuals with disabilities. But Medicaid is a means-tested program and is available only to those with very limited income and assets. Those receiving Medicaid benefits face a dilemma in considering work: if they work successfully, their income would likely disqualify them from receiving Medicaid coverage of the LTSS they need to work, yet they may not earn enough to pay for the services on their own. The implicit tax on working overwhelms earned income, even from high-paying jobs. Insurance can only work for this population if risks are broadly pooled and this is difficult in today's private markets.

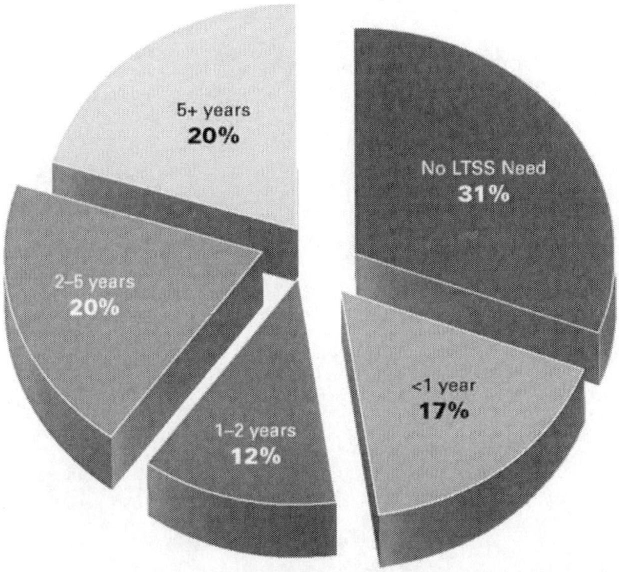

Source: Kemper, Komisar and Alecxih, 2005. Outputs of model using March 1993 and March 1994 CPS data.

Duration of Expected Future LTSS Need for Persons Turning 65.

- Older adults who need paid services may need them for varying lengths of time, depending on nature and onset of the condition and their life expectancy. Functional impairment is not an inevitable consequence of aging, and many older adults reach the end of their lives without experiencing a long spell of disability. A person turning 65 has a 20 percent chance of experiencing more than 5 years of ADL and IADL impairment requiring help from family or paid care in his or her remaining lifetime, but also has a 31 percent chance of dying without any serious long-term care need, and faces a 17 percent chance that needs will last less than a year.[67]
- Under current spending patterns, the expected value of all paid LTSS for a persone turning 65 in 2005 was $47,000, but the distribution of expenditures is highly skewed. Sixteen percent of the cohort could expect to use paid care valued at $100,000 or more over the course of their remaining years, and 12 percent could be expected to incur expenditures between $25,000 and $100,000. Forty-two percent of that cohort could expect no LTSS expenditures at all, either due to lack of need or exclusive reliance on informal care.[68]

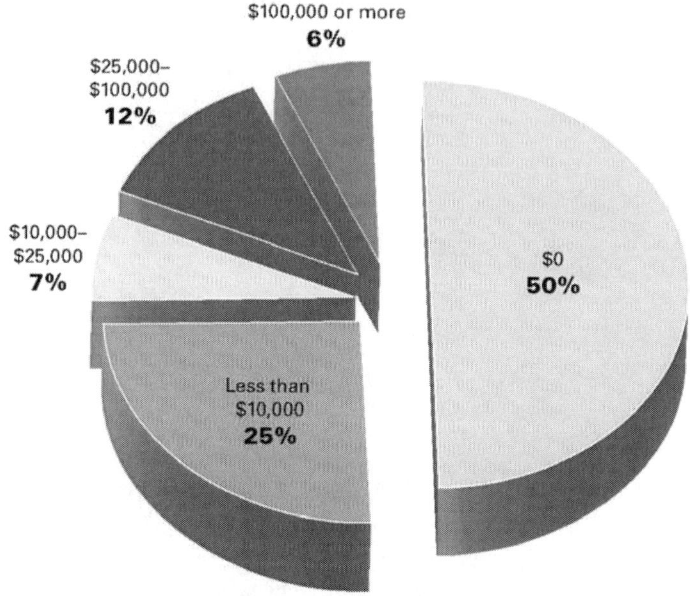

Source: Kemper, Komisar and Alecxih, 2005. Outputs of model using March 1993 and March 1994 CPS data.

Distribution of Future LTSS Expenditures for Persons Turning 65, All Sources.

- These varying amounts of paid LTSS are funded through a mix of sources with individuals and their families relying first on personal resources, including savings and private long-term care insurance when available, and then on multiple, uncoordinated public sources all with unique requirements, most notably Medicaid, a means-tested federal-state program. Each source of funding has constraints, and their interaction leads to further problems. The issues for each funding resource are different for younger persons with disabilities and older adults.

Personal Savings

- Individual income and assets are the first source for paid LTSS. However, many older adult households lack sufficient financial assets to provide for their LTSS. The inadequacy of many Americans' retirement wealth is well known: working-age individuals and families, facing competing and more immediate demands for spending or with few resources to save, do not save enough for retirement, let alone LTSS needs. Later, need for paid LTSS adds a further burden on retirement assets that are already strained. In 2005, only one in three older adults had non-housing financial assets equal to the yearly cost of nursing home care ($70,000).[69] The proportion was even lower for the subgroup that were more likely to require nursing home care due to age, family status or disability: only 16 percent held enough wealth to cover a year of care.[70] About 46 percent of older adult households have less than $10,000 in non-housing assets.[71] Given the unpredictability and catastrophic nature of extensive LTSS needs, relying on savings to finance these services is unlikely to be effective.

- Americans do not generally plan for future LTSS needs as they approach retirement. Sixty-five percent of Americans age 40 and up say they have done little or no planning even for ongoing living expenses in their older years— barely more than half know where to go for information on long-term care. Three in 10 Americans age 40 and older say growing older is something they "just don't want to think about," a sentiment especially expressed by those who worry about burdening their families, worry about being alone in their later years, lack confidence that they know where to turn to find information on the issue, and feel they lack the financial resources to pay for long-term care costs. Those who do not want to think about aging are less likely to plan for it. However, people who feel they know where to get information on aging issues are more apt than others to have prepared for these needs. Experience also matters: planning is significantly higher among the 53 percent of Americans age 40 and older who have themselves provided LTSS assistance to another person.[72]
- Experience to date suggests that, for generations retiring in the next few decades, there will be large numbers of older adults who will not have sufficient income and assets built up over working years to enable them to pay for a lengthy period of LTSS on their own.

Insurance

- Given the skewed incidence of functional impairments for older adults, with some people needing large amounts of services for a long duration and some needing none, it would seem that LTSS should be an appropriate area for insurance solutions.

- Private health insurance typically does not cover non-medical expenses beyond short-term, rehabilitation-oriented care. Likewise, Medicare, which provides universal coverage for people receiving Social Security Disability Insurance benefits (after a two-year waiting period) and for persons over age 65, does not cover long-term services and supports.
- While private long-term care insurance products have been sold for more than 30 years, any potential for them to serve a large percentage of the population has not been realized. Private long-term care insurance policies currently play a minor role in financing LTSS—only 10 percent of the potential market of Americans age 50 and above is currently insured.[73] New issuance of policies has declined in recent years, and a significant number of insurers have left the private LTCI market and closed blocks of policies due to low interest rates that have affected the products' financial performance, and unexpectedly low forfeiture rates, among other reasons.[74] Many policies that are in force have recently experienced substantial premium increases.[75]
- Issues on the demand and supply sides of the long-term care insurance (LTCI) market are responsible for the low penetration of private LTCI. The potential to benefit from Medicaid coverage deters ("crowds out") some people from purchasing LTCI, although analysts disagree on the significance of this effect.[76] Features of the products, the insurance market, and some regulatory requirements limit the value and attractiveness of private LTCI, including: underwriting standards that prevent many individuals from qualifying, high monthly premiums, policy forfeiture rules, limits on benefits, and a lack of public understanding and confidence in the private LTCI products.[77]
- Innovation with LTCI product designs has shown some promise of attracting more consumers. One approach—the Partnership for Long-Term Care—is an arrangement between states and private insurers that enables purchasers of LTCI to retain larger amounts of assets and still qualify for Medicaid after they have used their long-term care policy. The Partnership expanded after the Deficit Reduction Act of 2005 extended eligibility to all states and enabled policyholders to change states and retain the policy. Forty-five states now offer

Partnership plans. The number of policies, though still only 10 percent of LTCI policies, grew in recent years.[78] Surveys have shown that almost half of those surveyed would purchase LTCI if their state had a Partnership program, although most knew little about the program and were unaware that their state offered those plans.[79]

- Another promising approach is combination products that combine life insurance or annuities with long-term care insurance. Products like the Life Care Annuity can combine risks in ways that can make premiums more affordable and deliver more value to the consumer. The combination of the life annuity with long-term care insurance enables the insurers to issue the product with less underwriting.[80]
- The potential for savings and private insurance purchase to meet financing needs for LTSS has been limited by the proportion of the population with sufficient lifetime earnings and asset accumulation to pay for LTSS or to afford insurance purchase. New options and incentives making it practical for people to save or purchase insurance at lower levels of income could expand this market, enabling more people to prepare for their own LTSS needs.

Medicaid

- When individuals and families have exhausted their personal resources and can no longer shoulder LTSS costs on their own, they have to depend upon Medicaid for help. Individuals become eligible for Medicaid if they are eligible for Supplemental Security Income due to low incomes and assets, or as a result of spending down their incomes and assets on medical and LTSS expenses. Eligibility for Medicaid and the array of benefits provided vary substantially by state.
- Working-age adults with sufficient work histories may qualify for Social Security Disability Insurance (and Medicare after a two-year waiting period) and may be dually eligible for Medicare and Medicaid by virtue of having low incomes.[81] About 15 percent of Medicaid enrollees are dually eligible and about a third of these are under age 65 adults with disabilities. Two-thirds of Medicaid enrollees using LTSS are dual beneficiaries.[82]
- State Medicaid programs pay for the specific LTSS services specified by each state plan for people who meet the income and assets tests

particular to their state. Nursing home services must be offered, but other LTSS services are optional. Depending on state thresholds, older adults with low income and assets are likely to have been eligible for Medicaid before they experience LTSS needs. But some people become eligible for Medicaid due to their spending on paid LTSS: they "spend down" to Medicaid eligibility by spending nearly all their income and assets on services. Because nearly all income must be spent before Medicaid begins to pay, rules protect some income and assets for community-resident spouses. In addition, there are asset exclusions that enable a Medicaid recipient to retain working assets of substantial value. For example, the value of the family home is protected during the lifetime of the Medicaid recipient and spouse.[83]

- Some have suggested that individuals with high lifetime incomes may transfer assets to become Medicaid-eligible instead of planning for LTSS risk, and thus subvert Medicaid's purpose of serving the poor. However, a Government Accountability Office (GAO) study examining the impact of tightened asset transfer provisions enacted in the Deficit Reduction Act of 2005 found that most older adults gaining Medicaid eligibility have very limited incomes, and that asset transfers were both rare and generally modest in size, both before and after the new provisions.[84] There are competing views concerning the extent to which individuals can plan within current Medicaid rules to retain assets while achieving Medicaid eligibility.[85]
- Medicaid is the single largest payer for paid long-term services and supports. Today, Medicaid pays for 62 percent of paid LTSS while more than 22 percent is paid out-of-pocket, and other private payers pay for only 12 percent. In 2011, total spending for LTSS expenditures from all sources was $211 billion of which Medicaid expenditures account for $131 billion.[86] About half of Medicaid LTSS spending pays for services for persons under the age of 65.
- State Medicaid spending overall is putting pressure on state budgets now and is likely to overwhelm both state and federal budgets in the coming decades. However, only 30 percent of Medicaid spending is for LTSS; about half of this pays for nursing home services and the remainder pays for services provided in home and community settings.[87] A small percentage of Medicaid enrollees (6.4 percent) use LTSS, although this group (half aged and half disabled) account for nearly half (45.4 percent) of total Medicaid spending (counting both medical and LTSS expenses).

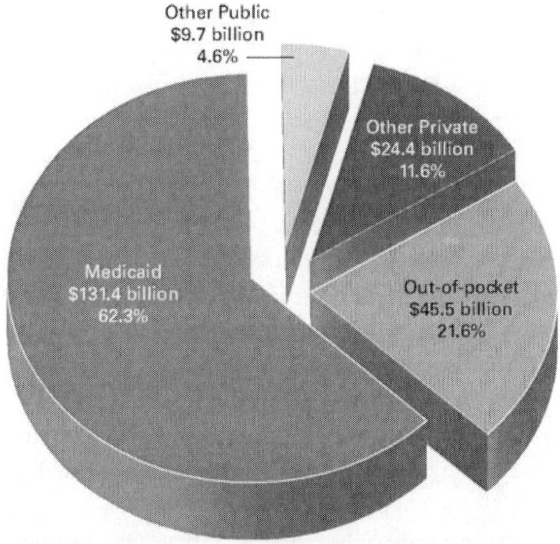

Source: National Health Policy Forum, based on data from 2011 National Health Expenditure Accounts.

LTSS Expenditures by Source, 2011.

- Medicaid LTSS spending has grown, but no faster than Medicaid's growth overall—about 5 percent a year since 2005. As a result, LTSS has remained a fairly constant share of total Medicaid spending.[88] On a per enrollee basis, Medicaid LTSS spending has grown only 0.1 percent a year since 2007.[89] Within total LTSS spending, however, spending on non-institutional services has grown substantially (from a third in 2005 to nearly half of total LTSS spending today) while spending on institutional services has remained fairly flat.
- Growing Medicaid spending competes with education and other state spending priorities. Moreover, the contraction of state tax revenues during the recent recession has put even more pressure on states to manage these costs. State spending on Medicaid accounted for 16.7 percent of all state general fund expenditures on average in 2011, roughly half the share that went to elementary and secondary education, consistent with its share over the preceding half decade. However, recently Medicaid's share of state budgets has been growing—from 14.8 percent in 2010 to a predicted 19.6 percent in 2012.[90]

- Total Medicaid spending is predicted to grow substantially over the next decade and put increasing pressure on federal and state budgets. The Congressional Budget Office (CBO) projects Federal Medicaid spending growth of 8 percent per year, rising from 1.7 of GNP today to 3.6 percent in 2037.[91] Much of this spending growth is expected to come from the addition of a population of previously uninsured adults and not from growing LTSS costs. CBO projects a 5.5 percent annual growth for LTSS spending in Medicaid, lower than the 8 percent annual growth rate CBO projects for Medicaid overall.[92]
- In response to growing budget constraints, almost every state has initiated Medicaid cost containment efforts. Over the last two years, almost all of Medicaid changes have focused on reductions in provider payments, with relatively few states initiating changes directly affecting LTSS users. Nevertheless, state budget pressures have influenced state decisions to seek Medicaid waivers to gain greater flexibility in eligibility and benefits to ensure appropriate targeting and to limit overall spending. In LTSS, Medicaid waivers have enabled states to implement HCBS for recipients who would otherwise qualify for institutional care, and to limit eligibility or cap slots for these services.

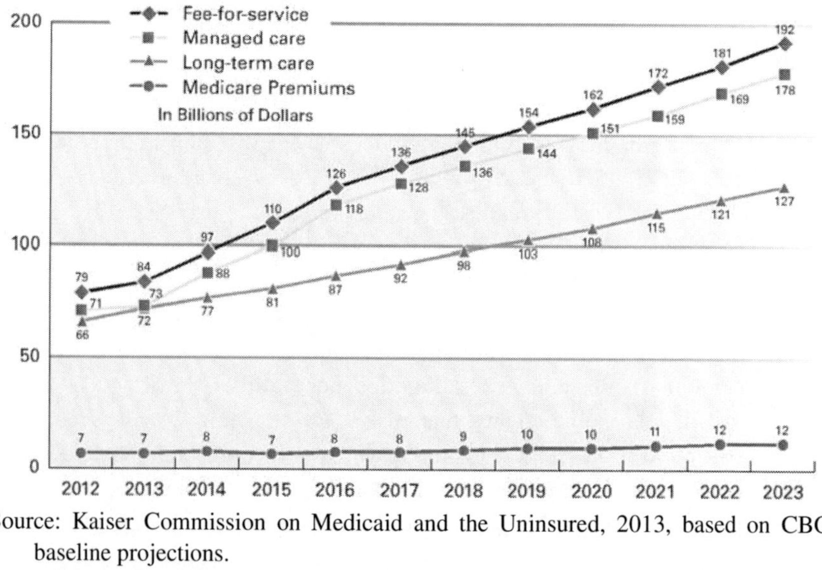

Source: Kaiser Commission on Medicaid and the Uninsured, 2013, based on CBO baseline projections.

CBO Federal Medicaid Spending Projections for Benefits 2012–2013.

- States are increasingly turning to contracts for LTSS with Medicaid managed care organizations as a means of containing LTSS costs and increasing coordination of services. In 2012, sixteen states were pursuing this strategy for at least a portion of their LTSS recipients, and a survey found that 11 additional states were planning to introduce this approach.[93] The programs are starting modestly, with only 389,000 enrolled by the end of 2012.[94] A number of the duals demonstration projects also use a contracted managed approach.

SECTION III. COMMISSION RECOMMENDATIONS

Part One – Service Delivery

Vision: A more responsive, integrated, person-centered, and fiscally sustainable LTSS delivery system that ensures people can access quality services in settings they choose.

Issue: Over 12 million Americans of all ages with functional impairments today receive long-term services and supports (LTSS) in their home and community or in an institution to assist them in performing daily activities of living. Family caregivers are the primary providers of these services and supports, but many individuals and their families rely on paid services for all or a part of their care. Many individuals and families pay for LTSS themselves or rely in part on coverage under private long-term care insurance they have purchased. Nearly a third of those receiving LTSS, however, rely on coverage under Medicaid. Medicaid, and the systems and providers it funds along with Medicare, are essential components of the network of services and supports for Americans with functional limitations. LTSS have improved substantially in recent decades and today most people with cognitive or functional limitations receive services and supports from dedicated caregivers and assistive technologies.

The process of accessing and navigating services, however, can be a tremendous challenge. People with cognitive and functional limitations today receive LTSS using a patchwork of family caregiving and publiclyand privately-funded assistance. The organization and delivery of services and supports is typically defined in terms of providers, settings, and funding streams rather than the needs of the person receiving assistance. Individuals and families in need of LTSS often lack a choice of services and supports that can meet their needs in the least restrictive setting.

The fragmentation and lack of coordination of the LTSS delivery system is due in part to the misalignment of benefit structures, conflicting rules, and separate funding streams of Medicare, Medicaid and other public and private programs. The lack of coordination is further compounded by an array of agencies, professionals and paraprofessionals that do not work together in an integrated, person-and family-centered way. In addition to access problems and the lack of consumer choice in the current system, individuals with cognitive and functional limitations and their family caregivers also experience disjointed care often disconnected from health care, housing, transportation and social services needed to support person-and family-centered LTSS.

LTSS are essential but costly for individuals with cognitive and functional limitations and their families. The array of confusing and poorly coordinated health care and LTSS creates a greater cost for individuals with cognitive or functional limitations, their families, and taxpayers than it should. Paying for needed LTSS is challenging for families facing severe financial pressures and for federal and state governments facing fiscal constraints and a growing need in the future for LTSS as the population ages and overall health care expenditures rise.

The current system of LTSS cannot meet the needs of a growing population in a time of severe fiscal constraints. Improvements in LTSS need to be developed with an appreciation for the economic challenges today and in the future and should include changes in the organization and payment for services. The application of new technologies can help improve health outcomes and lower the overall costs of LTSS and health-related services in the future.

Principles: The Commission believes that the LTSS delivery system should be organized to provide:

- A comprehensive array of person-and family-centered, high-quality, financially-sustainable medical and social services and supports that meets the heterogeneous needs, preferences and values of individuals with cognitive and functional limitations.
- Easy-to-access information and assistance for persons with cognitive and functional limitations and their caregivers to navigate the delivery system.

- Choice of settings and providers, the active involvement of individuals and family caregivers in making care decisions, and the delivery of services and supports that meet individuals' needs in the least restrictive setting consistent with their preferences.
- Integration of LTSS with medical and health-related care, including effective management of transitions between one type or level of care and another.
- Affordable, more efficient, coordinated health care and LTSS that aligns payment to reward providers for outcomes, quality of care and quality of life.

Recommendations

Rebalancing – A Balanced Array of LTSS

Recommendation: Promote services for persons with functional limitations in the least restrictive setting appropriate to their needs—building a system, including Medicaid, with options for people who would prefer to live in the community.

Problem:

- While states are mandated to cover nursing home and other institutional care, home and community-based services (HCBS) are an option funded only through a hodgepodge of waivers and state plan amendments.
- States primarily use Medicaid waivers to provide home and community-based services (HCBS) to recipients who would otherwise require institutional care. State variation in eligibility, services, limitations and caps results in very different levels of access to HCBS in different states. There are over 300 waivers providing for HCBS today. States have used waivers to limit access to the Medicaid services or impose enrollment caps and waive some income and asset rules and still retain the federal match. Many individuals who would otherwise qualify for HCBS are currently on state waiting lists for services or do not have access to services. The amount of service available to an individual once eligible for HCBS is also capped in terms of hours and state expenditures.

Detailed Recommendation:

- The Commission recommends that Congress incentivize state provision of care and services to enable individuals to live in the most integrated setting based on a person-centered process that is informed by an objective assessment of need.
  - CMS should ensure that evolving systems of care prioritize access to HCBS, based on individuals' needs, values, and preferences.
  - Ensure individuals and their family caregivers have access to information on choices of LTSS services to enable them to make informed choices between institutional and HCBS services.
  - Reduce Medicaid waiver complexity by streamlining the HCBS provisions of the Medicaid statute and having CMS provide technical assistance to the states in order to encourage rebalancing efforts.
  - Commission a study of the potential for savings across acute care and LTSS resulting from expanded access to HCBS for targeted populations due to more successful transitions from acute and post-acute care to community-and home-based care, and fewer unnecessary institutional admissions and readmissions.

Care Integration

Recommendation 1: Establish a single point of contact for LTSS on the care team.

Problem:

- Persons with cognitive and functional limitations and their families faced with a care transition—from an episode of acute care to an institutional stay or services in their home or in a homeor community-based setting— often find it difficult to identify and obtain access to the right services in the right settings and to navigate the confusing maze of requirements, agencies, and providers.
- Arrangements made for post-transition care may not be well coordinated with the medical care plan or sufficient to reduce the need for follow-on medical care or hospital readmission.
- A single point of contact—a personal navigator, case manager or care coordinator—for the individual with cognitive and functional limitations and primary caregiver can address issues that arise with

their LTSS needs. A medical professional who serves as the single point of contact with the medical care team alone is not sufficient for LTSS needs that are typically met through a separate care system not coordinated with the activities of the medical team.

Detailed Recommendation:

- The Commission recommends that certification and accreditation bodies adopt a standard for incorporating a LTSS single point of contact for persons with LTSS needs that is coordinated with or an integral part of the medical care team.

Recommendation 2: Align incentives to improve the integration of LTSS with health care services in a person-and family-centered approach.

Problem:

- LTSS has traditionally been provided in a fragmented, uncoordinated system of care provided by disparate agencies, each with its own funding, rules and processes, and which are separate from the health care system.
- Particularly for the two-thirds of persons receiving Medicaid LTSS benefits who are also Medicare beneficiaries ("dual eligibles"), the separate funding and provider silos have interfered with the coordinated care for an individual across the continuum of care.
- Successful integrated models that provide comprehensive, person-centered services across an array of settings (e.g., Program of All-inclusive Care of the Elderly (PACE)) have been small scale and have not been widely adopted.
- Demonstrations to test models to integrate care across the settings (e.g., CMS's Duals Demonstrations) and pioneering state efforts to develop innovative, high-functioning statewide LTSS systems (e.g., Minnesota and Washington), including projects to improve transitions from the hospital to home and community-based services, will only serve a small population in the short term.

Detailed Recommendations:

- The Commission recommends that CMS, the states, consumers, and the provider community work together to devise creative strategies to encourage a more rapid and widespread adoption of successful evidence-based person-and family-centered integrated care pilots.

- The Commission recommends that CMS's Accountable Care Organization (ACO) initiative and physician payment reforms focus on the whole range of LTSS needs of individuals and explore ways in the next round of experiments to expand the scope of the ACO's and new physician payment models to include coordination with LTSS providers.

Recommendation 3: Use technology more effectively to mobilize and integrate community resources and to share information among providers, individuals and family caregivers across settings of care.

Problem:

- Activity underway now to develop the platform for electronic health records (EHRs) does not currently incorporate the LTSS components of care in a way that would enable all care providers to have access to a unified care plan. LTSS are not included in "meaningful use" requirements and incentive programs that are shaping the contents of EHRs. Some states have begun to incorporate LTSS in state-level Health Information Exchanges (HIE) that enable providers to exchange health records for purposes of providing coordinated services.
- A variety of tele-health applications are already in use in LTSS and the related health care system. Others are under development. Emerging evidence shows that technology enabled-LTSS has the potential to increase team efficiency and effectiveness, enhance care coordination, promote quality of life, and improve outcomes such as reducing hospital admissions/readmissions and preventable injuries, such as falls. The biggest challenge has been to finance technology solutions in the context of relatively low-cost LTSS.

Detailed Recommendations:

- The Commission supports development by CMS and the Office of the National Coordinator for Health Information Technology (ONC) of an integrated HIT platform that would include LTSS (including incorporation of LTSS in Health Information Exchanges (HIEs), and recommends providing public resources necessary to support and accelerate the pace of this work.

- The Commission supports efforts to incorporate LTSS care plans in Electronic Health Records (EHRs) to enable providers to utilize a standardized care plan document as consumers with LTSS needs move among settings of acute care and LTSS.
- Family caregivers should be identified in the individual's EHR, especially when they are a part of the care plan. With the individual's permission, family caregivers should have access to such records as key members of care teams.
- The Commission supports efforts to innovate, test, and develop viable economic strategies for applying tele-health technologies to the LTSS system.

Recommendation 4: Create livable communities building on models that can improve access to services and health care-LTSS coordination.

Problem:

- Persons with LTSS needs require demand-responsive modes of transportation, accessible housing options, access to participate in employment, social and civic activities, as well as access to homecare services, clinics, and wellness programs.
- Few persons with LTSS needs today have access to livable communities (communities or neighborhoods that facilitate aging-in-place, personal independence, meaningful social engagement, and optimum health and well-being through approaches that share or arrange LTSS for people of all ages with functional limitations).
- The growing movement across America to create livable communities by mobilizing local residents, government, business and health care providers from the "ground up" to design and develop better places to grow old is still small scale. Successful models exist that are not replicated widely, including grassroots programs like the Village model, programs sponsored by charitable organizations or a combination of government and private-sector support like NORC-Supportive Services Program, Age-Friendly Communities, and commercial ventures by non-profit or religious organizations, like Continuing Care at Home.

Detailed Recommendation:

- The Commission recommends efforts to stimulate voluntary community efforts to create and sustain livable communities and aging-in-place support programs by establishing a national clearinghouse on successful practices, encouraging new model incubators that would provide small start-up funds and technical assistance, and undertaking further research and evaluation activities.

Uniform Assessment

Recommendation: Completion of a simpler and more usable standard assessment mechanism across care settings (acute, post-acute, and LTSS).

Problem:

- A tool to assess cognitive and functional capacity and LTSS needs is an essential component of effective care planning that ensures that services provided align well with an individual's needs, values, and preferences. A common or standard assessment tool across programs and services enables better alignment and coordination of care provided to the same individual from multiple programs and funding sources, and helps ensure consistent evaluation of need and provide data for evaluation of program performance and quality of care. However, the use of uniform assessment tools is rare within and across LTSS and health care providers.
- There is a wide array of tools for evaluating cognitive and functional capacity and LTSS needs (e.g., MDS, OASIS, MDS-Home Care). Yet, a CMS demonstration project to develop a single tool for Medicare post-acute patients did not result in implementation of the unified instrument across settings.
- Several assessment tools have been developed and used by various states for LTSS to determine eligibility, plan services and supports, and/or monitor quality. More than half of all states use a standard assessment tool for at least some portion of their LTSS populations, but these have not been adopted broadly for assessing HCBS need. Minnesota is creating a uniform, web-based assessment tool, to be implemented in June 2014, which is a comprehensive, person-centered, planning support tool that will be used for individuals of all ages, and with all types of disabilities (physical, cognitive, intellectual or other mental impairments) or other LTSS needs. The Minnesota

uniform assessment tool also assesses the needs of family caregivers through direct questions directed at the caregivers themselves.

- There is currently no single national assessment tool that applies across settings, services, and the full range of LTSS populations.

Detailed Recommendation:

- The Commission recommends the development and implementation of a standardized assessment tool that can produce a single care plan across care settings for an individual with cognitive or functional limitations. The standardized tool would inform consumers of LTSS choices and be responsive to the needs of older adults and all categories of individuals with disabilities in need of LTSS. The tool should:
  - Be used to inform LTSS choices by presenting service options based on individual's needs, goals, values, and preferences (not to close off LTSS options).
  - Be responsive to the needs of different populations (e.g., cognitive, intellectual, behavioral health, etc.).
  - Include the role of all providers and the needs of the family or other caregiver identified by the individual. Identify the caregiver in the uniform assessment and assess the caregiver's needs for training in the full care demands they are expected to perform.

Consumer Access/Assistance

Recommendation 1: Expand the "No Wrong Door" approach to provide enhanced options counseling for individuals to navigate LTSS, and provide the support needed to make this approach effective nationally.

Problem:

- Consumers have difficulty navigating the complex and confusing array of LTSS administered by multiple private and public agencies with complex and sometimes conflicting rules and regulations.
- "No Wrong Door" is a proven approach that assists consumers in identifying and qualifying for the appropriate services no matter where they enter the system—typically involving the cooperation of multiple agencies and organizations. It includes options counseling to assist families in making decisions about appropriate long-term care choices. There is considerable variation across the country in the

quality and level of services provided by ADRCs, and a lack of funding needed to improve their performance. CMS and the Administration for Community Living (ACL) developed extensive criteria and outcome measures for "fully functioning" ADRCs, and report that 80% of ADRCs have achieved more than half of the outcome measures. This indicates that many consumers are not served by fully functioning ADRCs, and are limited in services they receive.

Detailed Recommendation:

- The Commission recommends the expansion of the ongoing Enhanced ADRC Options Counseling Program, using states that are being funded now as national models, and relying on ACL and CMS to ensure best practices are disseminated to other states, and that other states receive support to expand their Options Counseling programs.

Recommendation 2: Provide information and assistance to consumers and family caregivers in advance of transition from one setting to the next (for example, acute care patients at admission not just at discharge).

Problem:

- Care transitions, such as a discharge from hospital or nursing facility, are often difficult and confusing for individuals with LTSS needs and their families. Individuals need access to information and assistance in exploring choices of possible support options in advance of discharge and at all hours. Inadequately prepared and supported transitions can result in unnecessary hospital admissions, readmissions, or institutionalization.

Detailed Recommendation:

- The Commission recommends the appropriate accrediting bodies review hospital policy on discharge planning and care transitions to ensure that discharge planning and risk assessment of the receiving setting occur at the beginning of an initial hospitalization or other precipitating event. Sources of information need to be developed that can provide timely (including after-hours) independent information in advance of discharge.

Recommendation 3: Improve access to information technology that can improve consumer and caregiver access to information.

Problem:

- Technological innovations can improve access to information and resources for older adults and individuals with disabilities.
- An example of the application of information technology is Minnesota's Senior LinkAge Line which provides information on Medicare, medications, LTSS, home care services, meal delivery, caregiver planning, and a host of other resources.

Detailed Recommendation:

- The Commission recommends that the ACL should establish a clearinghouse on information technology, and should support efforts to improve awareness and availability of such technologies for consumers and family caregivers.

Quality

Recommendation: Improve focus on quality across settings of LTSS—with particular attention to home and community-based services.

Problem:

- Nursing homes have been the primary focus of multi-faceted efforts to measure and improve quality for decades. Quality assessment and improvement efforts in nursing homes have not been translated to LTSS provided in home and community-based and other settings. Measurement of quality and appropriateness of services is important where recipients are dispersed and professional oversight is intermittent.
- Quality measurement is challenging for home and community-based services. Risk adjustment is a necessary component if measures are to be accepted and used as the basis for improvement efforts. HCBS measures should focus on outcomes, processes, utilization, and consumer and family experience.
- Efforts are currently underway to develop quality measures for home and community-based services. CMS has developed a set of quality domains and specified desired outcomes. The Measure Applications Partnership, convened by the National Quality Forum, is working to

certify measures for the state duals demonstrations. Of special interest are measures focusing on consumer experience as an outcome.

Detailed Recommendations:

- The Commission recommends increasing resources and accelerating the time frame for activities currently underway to:
  - develop quality measurement tools for use in home and community-based settings;
  - develop appropriate procedures and mechanisms for applying quality measures to ensure quality and appropriateness of services in these settings; and
  - develop measures on family experience of care, especially when caring for people with Alzheimer's disease or other cognitive or intellectual disabilities.
- The Commission recommends working with states to establish a system to publish quality measures that will be understandable to consumers, develop payment incentives and value-based purchasing of services based on quality after testing in pilot projects, and develop provider accreditation and certification based on quality.

Payment Reform

Recommendation: Advocate for new models of public payment that pay for post-acute and long-term services and supports on the basis of the service rather than the setting.

Problem:

- Historically, Medicare has paid for post-acute care based on phases of a beneficiary's illness as defined by a specific site of service, rather than on the characteristics or care needs of the beneficiary. Payments for the same consumer and services vary considerably across post-acute care settings.
- Providing "site-neutral" Medicare payment on the basis of the service provided across post-acute and LTSS settings would reduce incentives for serving individuals in more costly settings and could reduce Medicare (and possibly Medicaid) overall spending, realizing savings that could support HCBS and other LTSS.

Detailed Recommendation:

- The Commission recommends that necessary regulatory or legislative changes be made to adjust Medicare payment rates for post-acute services; and to test person-and family-centered payment models to include LTSS that would:
  - Pay providers based on the service provided to the consumer rather than site of care (while allowing for separation of the room and board components and capital adjustment for facility-based care).
  - Ensure beneficiaries are served where necessary care is available and provided. Settings that provide for highly specialized rehabilitation needs should be exempted and paid in a way that recognizes their special value.
  - Enable persons with cognitive or functional limitations to be served in the most cost-effective setting that can adequately deliver the most appropriate care.

Part Two – Workforce

Vision: An LTSS system that is able to support family caregivers and attract and retain a competent, adequately-sized workforce capable of providing high quality, person-and family-centered services and supports to individuals across all LTSS settings.

Issue: Family caregivers today provide the majority of LTSS. Those who take on this unpaid role risk the stress, physical strain, competing demands, and financial hardship of caregiving, and thus are vulnerable themselves. Due to declining birthrates that will result in fewer family caregivers than in years past, there could be greater reliance on fewer family caregivers and the availability and quality of paid caregivers will become increasingly important.

Direct care workers, whether working in residential settings or in a person's home, are often most familiar with the individual and his or her service needs, and are best able to provide services and supports in a person-centered way. Individuals with high levels of disability and complex health conditions increasingly receive LTSS in home and community-based settings, increasing the skill demands both for family caregivers and paid workers.

Many home care workers are employed by home care agencies, and many others are employed directly by individuals and their families, as personal care attendants under a Medicaid consumer-directed services program or as private household employees. Rarely do any of these workers receive adequate training to meet the demands of providing LTSS in a home setting, resulting in high rates of injury and high rates of turnover, reducing continuity of service. Low wages and few, if any, benefits with little opportunity for advancement compound to make it more difficult to retain a trained workforce. Growth of the older adult population and increasing integration of medical services with LTSS for all populations with cognitive or functional limitations will require more professional and direct care workers in LTSS settings, care planning, and participation in teams providing direct care.

Efforts to improve the availability and quality of paid and unpaid caregivers need to be framed in the context of the fiscal and economic pressures facing this country and the challenge of ensuring access to quality health care and LTSS for an aging population.

Principles: The Commission believes that workforce policy should follow the following principles:

- Family caregivers should be identified and assessed for their needs, especially when care plans are dependent on them, and they should receive the support they need to continue providing care to their loved ones.
- Paid direct care positions should hold the possibility of advancement and job satisfaction through career ladders and lattices.
- Competency evaluation should ensure that front-line care workers have the knowledge and skills they need to meet the assigned needs of the individuals in their care.
- The LTSS system should utilize both paid and family caregivers to their fullest potential by including them as integral members of care teams.
- Workforce policies should be designed to increase quality of care and retention of direct care workers.
- Sufficient numbers of health and social service professionals should be available to provide services connected with LTSS.
- Teams coordinating care for individuals with LTSS needs should include professionals who can address LTSS needs of individuals with

functional limitations, and are able to incorporate LTSS into the care planning for the individual.

Commission Recommendations

Family Caregiving

Recommendation 1: Maintain and strengthen a person-and family-centered LTSS system with both the person with cognitive or functional limitations and the family caregiver (spouse or partner, child or grandchild, parent, sibling, or other unpaid assistant) as a focus for services and supports. Include family caregivers and their needs in assessment and care planning processes.

Problem:

- Person-and family-centered care includes the individual with LTSS needs and his or her family at the center of the care team, and takes into consideration the individual's needs, preferences, cultural traditions, family situation, and values.
- Because family caregivers currently provide the majority of LTSS for individuals with disabilities, it is important that they be included in care planning and on the care team. Providers and professional caregivers can help ensure that family caregivers have the supports they need to continue caring for their loved one.
- Family caregivers are expected to perform complex medical/nursing tasks with little to no training and support from professionals.
- While there is a growing awareness that family caregivers need to be central in the care planning process, person-and family-centered care is practiced only to a limited degree.
- CMS, the Veterans Administration (VA), and ACL have identified a number of evidence-based transition interventions, many of which specifically include family caregivers in the intervention.

Detailed Recommendations:

- The Commission recommends that Congress require the Department of Health and Human Services (HHS) to develop a national strategy to support family caregivers, similar in scope to the national strategy developed to address Alzheimer's disease.

- The Commission recommends that CMS require assessment of family care-givers' needs and inclusion of family caregiver needs in a care plan or discharge plan that is dependent on them.
- The Commission recommends that CMS work with the VA and states to scale-up successful, evidence-based, person-and family-centered care and transition programs that effectively support individual's decision making and family caregivers.

Recommendation 2: Include family caregivers in patients' records and as a member of the care team.

Problem:

- Family caregivers already play an important role in the LTSS and medical care of their loved ones, serving as "de facto" care coordinators, and frequently performing nursing-level tasks such as medication management and wound care with little training.
- Many family caregivers of individuals with chronic conditions who play this role report feeling anxiety that they will make a mistake with medications, and that interacting with so many professionals and medical suppliers adds to their stress.
- Family caregivers providing wound care and managing medications for their care recipients reported that clearer instruction and training would make performing these tasks easier. These responses indicate that family caregivers should be offered appropriate training, be more integrated into care teams, and that communication between LTSS and medical professionals and family caregivers needs to be clearer.
- There is little information currently about the degree to which family caregivers are included as members of the care team, though advising bodies such as the Institute of Medicine have advocated for caregiver inclusion in care teams for some time, and the Office of the National Coordinator recently recommended that care team members, including family caregivers, should be listed on patients' medical records.

Detailed Recommendation:

- The Commission recommends that HHS and national accrediting bodies identify mechanisms that will encourage providers to integrate family caregivers into care teams and decision making.

Recommendation 3: Ensure family caregivers have access to relevant information through technology.

Problem:

- It is important that caregivers have access to all the information that they need to provide care, in addition to being listed on medical records.
- Development of caregiving technology has increased rapidly. Applications now allow users to track physiological conditions and symptoms/chronic disease management (blood glucose, blood pressure) and if individuals are pursuing their regular daily activities or if they may have fallen. New tools facilitate communication with health care and LTSS providers. Smart phone apps assist in a variety of caregiving functions. Assistive technologies increase mobility, the ability of individuals to accomplish daily tasks, and can improve communication.
- Research indicates that barriers remain for caregivers attempting to use health information technology to assist in caregiving. Mobile health applications do not yet support cognitive symptoms or brain health detection. Caregivers perceive cost of technology as a barrier to use, including the cost of assistive technologies. The general lack of awareness of these technologies is another barrier to more widespread use.

Detailed Recommendation

- The Commission recommends that HHS create a resource to disseminate information regarding new caregiving technologies and best practices for family caregivers, and provide local information about what is available to address their specific needs.

Recommendation 4: Encourage caregiver interventions, including respite options, and integration with volunteer efforts.

Problem:

- Respite care is the most commonly requested form of caregiver assistance; but respite must be addressed in the context of other forms of assistance provided by states, including information/assistance, education, and training and other caregiver support services.

- A number of federally-funded programs provide a limited amount of funding to states to provide caregiver support—including respite care. These include the National Family Caregiver Support Program, the Lifespan Respite Care Act, and the Alzheimer's Disease Supportive Services Program. The VA provides caregiver training systems for family caregivers of veterans. The resources provided by these programs are inadequate to meet the needs of all of these populations.
- Although researchers speculate that investing in respite care can result in cost savings by preventing caregiver burnout and the institutionalization of individuals who could have continued to receive care at home, most research to date shows mixed results in terms of impact on caregivers, delay of institutionalization, and cost effectiveness.

Detailed Recommendations:

- The Commission recommends further efforts to study caregiver interventions including respite care as part of a comprehensive approach to caregiver support, for their effectiveness in sustaining family caregiving and limiting the costs of most expensive institutional care.
- The Commission encourages an expansion of caregiver interventions based on evidence of their benefit, including volunteer efforts through a "caregiver corps" or modification of senior corps.

Paid Workforce

Recommendation 1: Revise scope of practice to broaden opportunities for professional and direct care workers with demonstrated competency.

Problem:

- Studies have documented the shortage of both professional and direct care workers for the care needs of older adults and persons with disabilities today and in the future.
  - Experts believe that expanding the roles of trained direct care workers may help compensate for the shortage in the professional workforce by allowing care to be provided more efficiently. This would permit taking full advantage of the capabilities of available workers, and would give professional workers more time to perform tasks for which only they are qualified.

- For example, allowing nurses to delegate to appropriately-trained direct care workers under their supervision tasks typically performed by nurses, such as administration of oral medications or injections, may result in more positive experiences for consumers.
- In addition, allowing direct care workers greater flexibility, respect, and responsibility has been shown to increase job satisfaction, which could have positive effects on retention of the workforce.
- One recent study of a pilot delegation demonstration in nursing homes found that all stakeholders, but particularly consumers, reported positive experiences with delegation.

Detailed Recommendation:

- The Commission recommends that states permit nurses to delegate and supervise certain tasks to direct care workers with sufficient training and demonstrated competency to perform them, particularly in home and community-based settings that do not have regularly scheduled registered nurses, subject to sufficient consumer protections.

Recommendation 2: Recommend that the federal government work with states to enable national criminal background checks for all members of the LTSS workforce.

Problem:

- No Medicaid program mandates criminal background check screening for all workers, although CMS does require states to report on their background check activities, if they choose to perform them. In addition, most states require criminal background checks on some LTSS workers, but there is significant variation in which workers are covered and which convictions preclude employment.
- Six states exclude family caregivers in consumer-directed programs from criminal background check requirements for workers providing services in the home.
- States can access multiple databases for background checks, including National FBI checks, state and county criminal records, state adult protective and child protective service registries, and sex offender registries, among others.

- However, the data systems available have many limitations, and states' ability to access data from other states is limited. In addition, a number of databases exist within each state, and they are often not integrated.

Detailed Recommendation:

- The Commission recommends that Congress direct the Department of Justice to examine barriers to sharing inter-state criminal background data for health care workers and accelerate efforts to develop solutions.

Direct Care Workforce

Recommendation 1: Create meaningful career ladders and lattices for direct care workers that result in access to career advancement opportunities and improved compensation.

Problem:

- Direct care worker positions are often viewed as low-wage, entry-level jobs with little to no opportunity for advancement. Establishing career ladders and lattices can increase the desirability of these positions, and improve job retention. [A lattice refers to a structure that allows workers to move laterally along a career path by developing specialized skill sets. A ladder, in contrast, allows workers to move upward by earning new credentials that build on prior experience.]
- A number of efforts have been made at the state and federal level to develop career ladders and lattices for direct care workers.
  - Extended Care Career Ladder Initiative (ECCLI) in Massachusetts: a competitive multi-round grant program available to nursing homes and home health agencies to develop career ladders and other training programs for nursing aides and home health aides that reported increased retention.
  - The Personal and Home Care Aide State Training (PHCAST) demonstrations administered by the Heath Resources and Services Administration—focused on the development of new training programs and curriculum centered on core competencies. Some states that have participated have incorporated career ladders and lattices into their training programs.

- CMS has also made efforts to identify core competencies among direct care workers across LTSS settings. These core competencies can be used to develop training programs, as well as career lattices and ladders.

Detailed Recommendation:

- The Commission recommends that, based upon the upcoming PHCAST evaluation, efforts should be made to identify best practices, and expand this program into other states, including successful career lattices and ladders.

Recommendation 2: Integrate direct care workers into care teams.
Problem:

- Direct care workers have a significant role in consumers' day-to-day lives and are often involved in health care activities (e.g., medication management, monitoring health status). Not giving direct care workers a significant role in interdisciplinary care teams limits the information available to the team on day-to-day care delivery and adherence and reduces the ability to coordinate with in-home assistance.
- Giving direct care workers integral roles in care teams has positive effects on consumer outcomes.
- A number of prominent care models, such as PACE or the Green House model, include personal care workers in their interdisciplinary teams.

Detailed Recommendation:

- The Commission recommends that CMS identify mechanisms to encourage providers to integrate direct care workers into care teams.

Recommendation 3: Recommend that the appropriate federal agency collect detailed data on the LTSS workforce.
Problem:

- Currently, there is a dearth of data on the direct care workforce. Although a number of states report worker shortages and high rates of turnover, they have little data available to assess the magnitude of the problem, and therefore find it difficult to address.

- A number of states are collecting data already, but none collect data across all settings in which workers work, and there is significant variation in which data they collect.
- Because states may use different terminology and use different means for classifying workers, data across states is not comparable.
- All states are required by OBRA 1987 to have CNA registries, but these datasets are designed to track certification processes and do not include adequate data about hours worked, wages, turnover rates, and workforce shortages.
- A recent CMS report on the subject suggested that states begin to collect data on the number of full and part time workers, turnover rates, vacancy rates, average hourly wages, and status of benefits for workers.
- Another challenge is that turnover is difficult to measure, and studies frequently use different methods to measure it, limiting the comparability of turnover data across studies.

Detailed Recommendation:

- The Commission recommends that the appropriate agency (e.g., CMS, Health Resources and Services Administration, Bureau of Labor Statistics) initiate a process to collect detailed data on the direct care workforce and launch comprehensive data collection efforts.

Recommendation 4: Encourage states to improve standards and establish a certification process for home-care workers.

Problem:

- Minimum training standards have been established by Federal regulation for nursing home certified nursing assistants (CNAs) and home health aides (HHAs). To meet Conditions for Participation in Medicare or Medicaid, workers holding these positions in skilled nursing homes or home health agencies respectively must meet these standards. Some states have established higher training standards. No Federal standards for training apply to home care workers providing Medicaid services.

- Currently, about a quarter of states either have state-sponsored curriculum for personal care attendants or require certification, but certification appears to be much more widespread for workers in institutional settings.
- The PHCAST demonstration requires that states develop certifications for trained and newly credentialed workers. The states involved in the demonstration differ in their approach to certification. While some have allowed the training organization to issue the certification directly, others plan to integrate the certification process into a state-wide process establishing a formal registry of direct care workers.
- The National Direct Service Resource Center within CMS has been developing core competency standards that apply to direct care workers across the care spectrum.

Recommendation:

- The Commission recommends that CMS explore the development of national training standards for direct care workers based on the outcome of the PHCAST demonstration in conjunction with CMS's effort to develop core competency standards or other model standards and certifications being developed by states. Following the approach taken with CNAs and HHAs in Medicare, CMS should explore ways for Medicaid to encourage states to apply training standards that at least meet minimum national standards.

Part Three – Finance

Vision: A sustainable balance of public and private financing for long-term services and supports (LTSS) that enables individuals with functional limitations to remain in the workforce or in appropriate care settings of their choice. One that (1) provides the tools and protections to enable Americans to comprehend and better prepare for the financial risk of needing LTSS; and (2) ensures that individuals with limited financial resources or for whom the cost of their care exceeds their financial resources have access to needed high-quality services and supports.

Issue: Americans are not adequately prepared for the magnitude of LTSS costs they could face as a result of their own aging or an extended period of physical or cognitive impairment. Nor are Americans, as taxpayers, ready to support the public cost of LTSS that will be exacerbated in coming decades by a growing aging and disability population, increased costs of care, and other factors.

Medicaid today finances 62 percent of all paid LTSS. Private savings and private long-term care insurance covers roughly a third of these costs. The looming retirement of tens of millions of baby boomers who have not acquired long-term care insurance or accumulated sufficient assets for potential long-term care needs, coupled with a decline in the availability of family caregivers, threatens to increase the reliance on Medicaid, to be financed by future taxpayers.

Expanded market penetration of private LTC insurance has been limited by the cost of coverage and medical underwriting, and is further hampered today by insurers reassessing the market due to unforeseen demographic and investment conditions. In addition, most people are unaware of the risks they bear for future LTSS needs, often falsely believing that Medicare or private health insurance will cover those costs. Finally, many workers today are not saving enough to maintain their standard of living in retirement, independent of any LTSS needs they may face. This lack of saving for future LTSS needs reflects not only more immediate competing concerns for today's workers but also a general difficulty in retirement saving.

To achieve a balance of public and private financing for LTSS and to assure that public resources continue to be available for those with the greatest need, more private resources must be accumulated to finance LTSS for a growing future population of individuals with cognitive and functional limitations. Without robust financial capacity from private LTC insurance and personal savings, Medicaid becomes the payer of last resort for the catastrophic LTSS costs of people who exhaust their resources paying for care.

Medicaid is a critical safety net program, but it is not designed to meet the LTSS needs of a diverse population. Its eligibility rules enable people who have earnings or other resources to qualify for LTSS, but only after spending down nearly all of their income and assets they need to remain independent. Younger workers with disabilities who need LTSS to enable them to work, often fall in the gap between making too much to qualify for Medicaid and too little to pay their LTSS costs. The tremendous state-by-state variability of Medicaid eligibility and benefits makes qualifying for benefits an uncertain exercise with uneven results across the country. Lack of clarity about public, private-sector, and individual responsibilities in financing LTSS adds to the uncertainty about the responsibilities of individuals and their families for supporting their LTSS resource needs.

Principles: Public policy toward the financing of LTSS must reflect a comprehensive and balanced approach to public and private responsibility. It must encourage and enable individuals to prepare adequately to finance their own needs while providing a strong safety net for those whose simply cannot do so.

An effective, publicly-funded safety net is essential for those with limited lifetime resources, including those whose physical, intellectual, or cognitive disabilities originate early in life. Medicaid must be improved to better provide needed LTSS to enable people to have more choice of person-and family-centered services that meet their needs, and promote opportunities for persons with disabilities to engage in meaningful work.

Although for most people the risk of needing a protracted period of LTSS is an insurable risk, this risk is not widely insured today. People who exhaust their resources end up using public support for costs that could have been insured either publicly or privately. Insuring these most devastating costs through catastrophic insurance would make clearer to individuals what they have to cover through savings and insurance. Policy interventions that provide or enable catastrophic insurance might well encourage Americans with modest financial resources to strengthen preparation for their LTSS needs through a more robust private insurance and personal savings. In turn, public policy changes to make long-term care insurance (LTCI) products more affordable and attractive, including allowing more variety in the structure of policies, would encourage private LTCI purchase.

The Commission considered very different approaches regarding the mechanisms needed to make this vision possible. The Commission did not agree on a financing approach, and, therefore, makes no recommendation. The Commission is instead offering two different approaches presented by members of the Commission (below) to illustrate ways the Congress could achieve a restructuring of LTSS financing. In doing so, we seek to achieve a better balance of public and private resources, improve financial protection from the risk of LTSS expenses in coming decades, and better prepare those in future generations who can prepare for the potential expenses of LTSS.

Regardless of the policy approach adopted, the Commission believes Americans are more likely to adequately prepare if they have a clearer understanding of the risk of needing LTSS, the interrelated public and private mechanisms for financing that risk, and access to reliable and affordable tools they need to do so.

Alternative Approaches

Approach A: Strengthen LTSS financing through private options for financial protection

Problem:

- Governments are facing serious budget constraints that threaten funding for existing health care, disability, and retirement programs. We cannot assure the safety net will hold for the most vulnerable who must rely on public programs if we also publicly finance care for millions of Americans who could prepare now for their needs in future years.
- Private long-term care insurance (LTCI) could play a more substantial role in LTSS financing, but changes are needed to boost participation, including new incentives, more flexibility so insurers can offer greater variety in the structure of policies and make coverage more affordable, and educational campaigns to explain future risks and options for financial planning.
- Creative solutions are needed to bring together new partnerships, new incentives, and innovative programs for those who can prepare now for their own long-term care needs to make sure the public safety net is there for those most in need. Private savings and a diverse choice of products are critical components of the LTSS financing solution.

Proposal:

- Provide new market incentives: Fewer people are purchasing long-term care insurance policies today, and fewer companies are offering the policies. The high cost of policies is a primary deterrent. A lack of understanding about the risks of not having financial protection and the lack of incentives to purchase coverage also contribute to limited uptake of LTCI.
    - Provide a tax preference for long-term care policies through retirement and health accounts: Allowing withdrawals from existing 401k, IRA, or Section 125 accounts to pay LTCI

premiums or distributions would have minimal tax implications. The tax costs of incentivizing broader participation would be more than offset over time as those with private coverage draw on private rather than public resources to finance their care.

- Support new forms of combination policies such as a "life care annuity," which combines a life annuity insurance policy with long-term care insurance: A change in tax law to allow investment and distribution in the LTCI portion through tax-advantaged retirement accounts would encourage creation and uptake of these policies. The combination policy reduces adverse selection in the immediate life annuity portion, resulting in lower premiums, and allows for considerable relaxation in underwriting standards for the long-term care portion of the policy.
- Support Long-Term Care Partnership Programs that currently operate in most states: These public-private partnerships allow residents to purchase long-term care insurance and still qualify for Medicaid if and when their insurance is exhausted without depleting all of their assets. The program combines the benefits of private insurance with the backing and safety net of the government.
- Allow a Medicaid Carve Out: individuals would have the option (when claiming Social Security retirement) of receiving a portion of the expected actuarial present value of Medicaid benefits, adjusted down by income, as a subsidy to purchase permanent long-term care insurance, including through combination policies. In exchange, they would give up the right to future Medicaid LTC services.
- Provide protection for catastrophic LTC costs: Create a financing mechanism for the catastrophic "tail" of costs (the small number of long-durational, high-cost LTSS) not now covered by private LTCI. This would combine a safety net for truly catastrophic costs, through private or public reinsurance, with private responsibility (savings, family care, and private LTCI).
- Remove regulatory burdens and barriers: regulatory inflexibility has hampered the ability of carriers to respond to rapid and large changes in the economy and to provide affordable and attractive products to consumers.
- Allow flexibility in pricing and product design: rapid and sustained drops in interest rates induced by unusual Federal

Reserve monetary policies have challenged LTCI carriers expecting a more traditional return on investment. Private LTCI carriers need greater flexibility in structuring policies, including policies with varied benefit structures (e.g., longer elimination periods) and benefit time periods, to continue to meet consumer needs for affordable policies.
  - Allow LTCI policy portability: allow policy portability through such mechanisms as multi-state compacts, possibly developed in consultation with the National Association of Insurance Commissioners.
  - Minimize Medicaid Crowd-Out: The structure of federal health care programs, particularly Medicaid, discourages individuals from taking responsibility for their future long-term care needs. Medicaid resources need to be more carefully targeted to those individuals the program was intended to serve—the needy and the poor.
  - Strengthen Medicaid eligibility requirements for middle-income Americans: Consider retirement assets and a larger portion of home values for those applying for Medicaid.
  - Strengthen asset recovery: Ensure states meet their responsibility to oversee and enforce asset recovery to prevent middle- and upper-middle income seniors from hiding assets to gain eligibility for Medicaid.
  - Use reverse mortgages: Use reverse mortgages to enable seniors to use the value of their home equity to fund long-term care services, including while remaining in their homes. Enable retirees to pre-qualify so funds would be available when needed.
- Education:
  - Establish an ongoing awareness campaign: Educate the public about the limitations of Medicare and Medicaid in funding LTSS and the options and incentives for private financial protection.

Approach B. Strengthen LTSS Financing through Social Insurance

Problem:

- The LTSS crisis is a societal problem that requires a societal solution. The need for LTSS is an unpredictable, catastrophic risk for people under and over age 65. Responsible individuals and families cannot plan for exigencies such as illness, accident, or advanced age that create LTSS needs or pay for services when those needs arise.

- America does not have a LTSS financing system that provides a comprehensive, coordinated, reliable structure for people in need of long-term care; it has an area of disparate public and private payment mechanisms.
- Currently, the only way to finance care over the long term is to either qualify for Medicaid or have enough resources to purchase long-term care insurance and/or self-insure. Neither Medicaid nor private insurance is certain to meet an individual's LTSS financing needs. Medicare is a social insurance program, but it only covers post-acute care and does not cover children and individuals who have not worked sufficiently to qualify.
- A social insurance approach provides a public financing mechanism that spreads risk broadly, sharing the costs between the government, participants, and /or employers and employees. Since everyone is at risk, everyone contributes in order to benefit should a long-term functional need arise. Mandatory participation makes the risk pool viable.
- Insuring a portion of the risk for everyone through social insurance allows those who have resources to assume responsibility for the uninsured portion through personal savings, private insurance, or other mechanisms.

Proposals—Two Possible Social Insurance Models

1. Create a Comprehensive Medicare Benefit for LTSS

- Include a comprehensive LTSS benefit in Medicare Part A that would be triggered, like the hospice benefit, when an individual is certified to meet certain qualifying criteria.
- Qualification for the LTSS benefit would be based on a physician certification that the individual requires assistance with at least two activities of daily living, has needed such assistance for 90 days, and is likely to continue to need the services. Individuals could qualify equally based on certified ongoing and continued cognitive or mental health issues such that independence is impossible or contraindicated.

- The LTSS benefit would be financed through a combination of an increase to the current Medicare payroll tax and the creation of a Part A premium.
- Qualifying individuals would be eligible for reasonable and necessary LTSS services that would include: Skilled nursing facility care or daily skilled care; home health care without the need for a skilled service; personal care attendant services; care management and coordination; adult day center services; respite care options to support family or other volunteer caregiver; outpatient therapies; other reasonable and necessary services.
- Since not all people with LTSS needs are eligible for Medicare, consideration should be given to including those who meet the agreed-upon benefit criteria but would otherwise not be part of the Medicare program. In the alternative, other social insurance funding should be developed to meet these individuals' needs.

2. Create a Basic LTSS Benefit within Medicare or a New Public Program

- This approach would create a more limited benefit, either within Medicare or as a new public program, to insure only catastrophic risk and making clear the "hole" that people able to prepare in advance should plan to fill through private resources.
- People assessed as meeting a specified threshold of functional impairment would qualify for benefits after a waiting period. The length of the waiting period (shorter for people with lower incomes and becoming longer at higher incomes) would be established at or near retirement age and tied to Social Security-reported income, averaged over a number of years. For younger people who become impaired, the formula relating waiting periods to income would be appropriately adjusted to reflect the lesser accumulation of resources at younger ages.
- To make the benefit available to people currently in need of assistance, an alternative to the proposed waiting period would be necessary, since private insurance to fill it may be unavailable or prohibitively expensive and people may lack the means to otherwise protect themselves. A broadly inclusive benefit would therefore replace the waiting period with an income/asset-related deductible for people who, at the time the new benefit is established, have significant disabilities or are age 75 or older.

- Benefits under this arrangement would be specified as a dollar amount per day, vary with level of impairment and be applicable to the full range of LTSS services. Individuals could opt for a service rather than a cash benefit.
- Benefits could be financed through a combination of Medicaid savings (federal only or federal and state) and a surcharge on the income tax (higher for people currently near or at retirement age).

Neither of these social insurance models eliminates the private part of the public-private LTSS partnership. On the contrary, they mitigate risks and create a clear and manageable role for private insurance. To support supplementary or gap filling, new regulations are needed for the private long-term care insurance market to, at a minimum:

- Standardize and limit the types of policies insurers can offer, as in the Medigap market, in order to facilitate comparison and competition.
- Create an electronic market and provide information and direct assistance to consumers in order to facilitate comparison shopping and educated choices.
- Create effective consumer protections to ensure people receive fair value and promised benefits.
- Create easily accessible, meaningful appeals to those who are denied coverage or other rights afforded by their social or private insurance.

Social insurance would not cover all service needs or eliminate the need for personal financial contributions of family care or eliminate the need for an adequate public safety net—whether within it or through a continued (albeit much smaller) Medicaid program.

Recommendations

Medicaid Improvement

Recommendation 1: Create a demonstration project to provide workers with disability coverage for the LTSS they need to remain employed.

Problem:

- Individuals with disabilities often need personal assistance, mobility devices, assistive technology, or other LTSS in order to work and live independently. The cost of these supports greatly reduces the net benefits of paid employment and can be a barrier to a person with disabilities entering or remaining in the labor force.

- Workers with disabilities may or may not have access to health insurance through their employment. For those that do, employer-provided health insurance rarely covers the cost of LTSS.
- Medicaid provides LTSS to individuals with disabilities based on eligibility for the Supplemental Security Income (SSI) disability program. The SSI income limits prevent a worker with a substantial disability from qualifying for Medicaid if they earning more than roughly 250 percent of the federal poverty level.
- Consequently, those receiving SSI benefits face a dilemma in trying to work: If they work successfully, their income would likely disqualify them from receiving Medicaid LTSS, yet they may not be earning enough to pay for the services entirely on their own.

Detailed Recommendation:

- The Commission recommends that Congress authorize a demonstration project (under section 1115 of the Social Security Act) to test the feasibility of providing LTSS to those who work despite having a significant disability. The project would:
  - Target workers with a severe disability (that meets or equals Social Security's medical listings) but whose income from work precludes SSI or SSDI eligibility
  - Provide LTSS that can wrap around employer-provided health benefits
  - Include worker cost sharing that would be graded with amount of income

Recommendation 2: Assist the states to achieve greater uniformity of eligibility and benefits in State Medicaid Buy-In programs for LTSS for workers with significant disabilities.

Problem:

- Working-age adults with disabilities who need LTSS, such as personal assistance, mobility devices, or assistive technology, to enter or remain in the workforce do not have health insurance that will cover the LTSS.

- The Medicaid Buy-In program was created to enable working adults with disabilities whose income and assets would otherwise make them ineligible for Medicaid coverage to pay premiums to "buy into" Medicaid for its LTSS coverage.
- The two federal laws creating the Medicaid Buy-In (the Balanced Budget Act and the Ticket to Work and Work Incentives Improvement Act) impose different rules around issues such as income limits, premiums, and the treatment of employment interruptions; and State programs vary in how they apply these rules.
- Disabled workers are limited in their mobility to pursue job opportunities by the risk of losing their Medicaid coverage for their LTSS expenses if they move to another state.

Detailed Recommendation:

- CMS should assist states in developing a more uniform Medicaid Buy-In program that would allow individuals with significant disabilities to remain attached to the labor market and optimize employment opportunities, including those that may require moving to another state.

Medicare Improvement

Recommendation 1: Eliminate the three-day hospital stay requirement for SNF coverage.

Problem:

- Medicare covers acute hospital and limited post-acute care. It does not cover long-term services and supports. Medicare will pay for skilled nursing facility care only after a prior hospitalization lasting at least three days. Medicare then pays the full cost of the nursing home stay for the first 20 days and a portion of the cost after for up to 100 days total.
- The three-day prior hospitalization requirement was implemented shortly after Medicare's enactment. The three-day requirement, along with the cap on nursing home days, is intended to limit the use of Medicare in funding skilled nursing care. Congress eliminated the three-day rule in 1989 in a law that was later rescinded, leaving the rule intact.

- With declining hospital lengths of stay, many inpatient stays that require post-acute skilled nursing may not qualify for coverage. Also, in recent years, hospitals have been holding increasing numbers of patients in "observation status," rather than admitting them as inpatients. Recently, CMS has been allowing hospitals to retroactively recode inpatient stays as "observation status."
- Without the three-day inpatient stay, patients who should be transferred for a short post-acute stay in a skilled nursing facility cannot get coverage for the stay unless they are also eligible for Medicaid. Failure to transfer patients who need rehabilitation in a skilled nursing facility may increase unnecessary hospital readmissions.

Detailed Recommendation:

- The Commission recommends enactment of legislation to eliminate the requirement of a prior three-day inpatient stay in a skilled nursing facility.

- The Commission recommends that CMS count stays in observation status toward the meeting the prior three-day hospitalization requirement for SNF coverage until such time as the statute is changed to remove the requirement.

Recommendation 2: Reconsider the requirement for receiving home health services under Medicare that the individual be "homebound."

Problem:

- Medicare requires that an individual be "homebound," need intermittent skilled nursing care, and be under a physician's plan of care to qualify for home health and therapy services.
- An individual is considered "homebound" if he or she cannot leave home without "considerable and taxing effort," which includes requiring the aid of supportive devices, the use of special transportation, the assistance of another person, or has a medical condition for which leaving the home is contraindicated.
- An individual can leave the home without assistance without being disqualified for services if the absence is for:

   - medical or therapeutic and psychosocial treatment, or
   - a non-medical purpose that is "infrequent or short in duration," such as attending a religious service, trip to a hairdresser, special family event, or walk around the block.
- For Medicare beneficiaries who could use the Medicare home health benefit to meet their long-term needs, the limitation to certain short and infrequent trips imposes a difficult lifestyle burden. Beneficiaries who could leave their home if they obtain home care are either trapped in their homes or have to find an alternative way to meet their care needs.

Detailed Recommendation:

- The Commission recommends that CMS revise the homebound requirement to ensure it does not create inappropriate barriers to care and to assess the cost implications of doing so.

Savings

Recommendation: Allow individuals and families with significant disabilities to access the educational savings program to assist in saving for a current or future LTSS need.

Problem:

- Section 529 of the Internal Revenue Code allows families to set aside funds for future college expenses in an education savings account operated by a state or educational institution, allowing the principal to grow tax deferred and exempting distributions for college costs from tax.
- Parents of children with disabilities want their children to have access to higher education, have a pathway to a meaningful career, and save for the future so that they can live independently. Adults with disabilities also want to accumulate assets so that they too can live independently.
- An expansion of IRC section 529 would allow individuals with disabilities or their families to set funds aside in a tax-advantaged savings account, up to $100,000, so that funds could be withdrawn to cover costs of health care, employment support, housing, transportation, the purchase of technology, and education.

Detailed Recommendation:

- The Commission recommends that Congress amend Section 529 of the IRS code to allow individuals and families with significant disabilities living with LTSS needs who are not receiving assistance from the Medicaid program to have access to an established program designed to assist individuals and families to save for an educational need and to also save for a current or future LTSS need.

SECTION IV: ADVANCING AN AGENDA ON LONG-TERM SERVICES AND SUPPORTS

Recommendation 1: Create a subsequent national advisory committee to continue this work and consider the Commission's recommendations and potential financing frameworks as a starting point for its own assessments and recommendations.

Problem:

- The breadth and depth of issues encompassing long-term services and supports, the magnitude of its impact on American families now and in the future, as well as its cost implications on private and public resources all dictate the need for a sustained national dialogue on the subject.
- While the constitution of this dialogue could take several forms, several reasons listed below necessitate, in our view, the creation of a longer-tenured national committee that includes both governmental and private-sector stakeholders along with consumer and family caregiver representatives and LTSS service recipients.
  - The need for designing, executing and financing LTSS is of major continuing importance to the health and quality of life of millions of Americans today and tens of millions of Americans in the future. An effort to find substantial consensus on these elements will require sustained focus, conversation, and additional analysis.
  - There is dynamic change in our country's health care payment and delivery systems, technology, health and supportive service structures, behaviors and performance, and demographics

requiring ongoing evaluation of the models being tested at the local, state, and federal levels for those that can be taken to scale.

- The costs to and burdens on Americans—both as individuals and taxpayers—for LTSS for the large and growing population of those with functional and cognitive impairments needing such services will place increasing stress on American families and the nation's fiscal health.
- Increasing the availability and quality of paid caregivers is critical to meeting the needs of this growing population as is the strengthening of mechanisms to support family caregivers, who will remain a mainstay support for many, if not most, of those with LTSS needs. Ongoing evaluation and promotion of new technologies and best practices in the monitoring of LTSS service needs and delivery as well as training of unpaid and paid caregivers, will be necessary.
- The ability to integrate LTSS into our rapidly changing health and supportive services environment in light of the capacities for both human and technological capital requires persistent and consistent engagement by Executive and Legislative branch officials as well as leaders in the health and supportive service sectors and representatives of consumers, caregivers, and those with LTSS needs.

- The current Commission on Long-Term Care, working within its budget, operational structure, and statutorily defined timelines, deliberated on many of these items in its less-than-100-day working period. Section Three includes a series of recommendations and potential financing frameworks that begins to address these issues. Having said that, this Commission recognizes that its work is not the end of the road for the consideration of all of the issues implicated by the needs and demands for a more responsive and better financed LTSS system.

Detailed Recommendation:

- The Commission recommends that a subsequent national advisory committee be created to continue this work and consider the Commission's recommendations and potential financing frameworks as a starting point for its own assessments and recommendations. This advisory committee should be positioned and composed so it can effectively engage with and appropriately leverage the existing federal knowledge and resources that exist on this topic, which operate within and across several departments (i.e., HHS [including the Social Security Administration], Education, Labor, Veterans Affairs, Transportation, Justice, and Treasury). The advisory committee should also receive analytic support from and coordinate with the congressional advisory bodies on Medicare and Medicaid (i.e., Medicare Payment Advisory Commission and Medicaid and CHIP Payment and Access Commission) as well as the key congressional and Administration budgetary and accounting bodies (i.e., CBO, Office of Management and Budget, and GAO).

- The charge of this new committee should be to assess, report on an ongoing basis and, where appropriate, recommend actions to achieve the following results:
  - Service Delivery: Create a more responsive, integrated, person-centered, and fiscally sustainable LTSS delivery system that ensures people can access quality services based on their needs, values, and preferences.
  - Finance: Ensure provision of a sustainable and integrated range of public and private financing mechanisms to meet the needs of people with functional and cognitive impairments.
  - Workforce: Attract and retain a competent, adequately sized, and sustainable workforce capable of providing high-quality, person-centered support to people across a variety of settings.
  - Caregiving: Provide information and services needed to maintain the physical and emotional health, safety, and financial stability of American families seeking to provide LTSS to their family members and friends.
  - Education: Develop an effective educational program about the availability of public and private financing of long-term care.

Recommendation 2: Convene the White House Conference on Aging to include LTSS.

- The Commission recommends convening the White House Conference on Aging in 2015 in coordination with the National Council on Disability to allow for the participation of states and other constituents in the continued focus on LTSS improvements.

APPENDIX A. COMMISSIONER IDEAS

A. Financing Ideas

Multi-Faceted

1. **Reconfiguring LTSS financing to share responsibility and enhance protection** Goal: To build a financing framework that (a) provides meaningful protection against the risk of costly long-term care; (b) is, to the extent possible, pre-funded by future users; and (c) includes significant personal responsibility, an effective insurance market, and a strong safety net.

   Premises:

   - The need for expensive, extensive LTSS is an unpredictable, catastrophic risk that, like similar risks, can be most efficiently and effectively met through insurance.
   - Private insurers face enormous difficulties in addressing this risk and, even with supportive public policy interventions and possible expansions (short of required purchase), can reach only a modest share of the population.
   - A limited public insurance program can establish a financing framework that encourages the purchase of private insurance.
   - Given responsible limits to public as well as private insurance, a public safety net will always be essential to assure access to adequate care for people with inadequate resources.

Proposal:

A. Establish a basic public LTSS benefit available to people assessed as meeting a specified threshold of functional impairment after a waiting period of up to x years. The length of the waiting period (shorter for people with lower incomes and becoming longer at higher incomes) would be established at or near retirement age and tied to Social Security-reported income, averaged over a number of years. For younger people who become impaired, the formula relating waiting periods to income would be appropriately adjusted to reflect the lesser accumulation of resources at younger ages. Benefits would be specified as a dollar amount per day, vary with level of impairment, and be applicable to the full range of LTSS services. Individuals could opt for a service rather than a cash benefit. With this type of benefit, people would know throughout their working years the risk or "hole" they should plan to fill (or the protection they might want to supplement) from personal resources or private insurance should they become impaired. The benefit could be financed through a combination of Medicaid savings (federal only or federal and state) and a surcharge on the income tax (higher for people currently near or at retirement age).

B. To supplement public coverage, create an effective private insurance market (for background and rationale, see Richard Frank, Mark Cohen and Neale Mahoney; http://www.thescanfoundation.org/sites/thescanfoundation.org/files/tsf_ltc-financing_private-options_frank_3-20-13.pdf.)
   1. Standardize and limit the types of policies insurers can offer, as in the Medigap market, in order to facilitate comparison and competition.
   2. Create an electronic market and provide information and direct assistance to consumers, in order to facilitate comparison shopping and educated choices.
   3. Require that alongside current level premium products, insurers offer people under age 65 products that index premiums and benefits in time blocks and apply "term pricing" (i.e., charge an annual premium covering the expected claim costs for a specified "term," say of 1–5 years, rather than for a lifetime—in order to engage younger people in the purchase of long-term care insurance and provide them lower premiums that reflect their own disability risks.
   4. Established reinsurance arrangements, financed by private insurers, that establish parameters for risk management and mitigate risks to individual companies.

C. To address current LTSS inadequacies and inequities across states as well as the unequal burdens of aging, strengthen the Medicaid safety net with enhanced federal financing (for background and rationale, see Judy Feder and Harriet Komisar, http://www.thescanfoundation.org/sites/thescanfoundation.org/files/Georgetown_Importance_Federal_Financing_LTC_2.pdf.)
   1. Gradually increase federal financing for Medicaid long-term care benefits from existing match percentages to 100 percent.

2. Define a nationally uniform benefit (imbedded in a mandatory personal care benefit and including an increase in the personal needs allowance) to vary with an individual's level of impairment, as determined standardized assessment process. Provide federal match at current rates to states choosing to supplement the federal benefit.
3. Set federal payment rates to providers, adjusted for geographic variation in input costs.
4. Finance the new benefit in part with state contributions (as in Medicare Part D)—set initially to reflect their current long-term care spending (up to a maximum) and indexed to reflect inflation and economic growth; the index would hold states "harmless" for increased demand associated with the aging of the population.

Moving forward:

The framework presented here is by no means a substitute for a variety of other policy changes we have discussed—including policies affecting younger people with disabilities, informal caregivers and the direct care workforce, care delivery, prevention, community initiatives, and existing Medicare and Medicaid payment, quality, assessment or other policies. Rather, it offers an over-arching financing strategy that can accommodate those improvements—the "comprehensive" part of the strategy in our mandate.

Furthermore, as a framework it is an outline, not a full proposal. Clearly it requires more detail, refinement, and analysis to move forward. Some of that can occur with the help of commission members and staff, but its full development will require post-commission work—as is likely also true for other proposals. As we've discussed, a call for that work should be part of this and other recommendations.

Finally—although I've written this proposal in a way that, I hope, facilitates understanding of its intent and architecture, my recommendation is that the timing of its implementation (and likely its legislation), start with step 3.

- The highest priority should go to preservation and enhancement of the safety net for people who are most disadvantaged, which is currently at risk.

- Adoption of a long-term strategy for long-term care financing will be a long-term struggle to which we should not hold this population hostage.

2. **Create a voluntary Medicaid carve-out program using adequate and permanent private LTCI policies.**
Motivation: Theoretical and empirical evidence point to a significant crowdout effect from Medicaid significantly reducing the role of private LTCI in financing LTSS. This effect increases government expenditures now and increasingly in the future, providing public insurance to many households in the middle class and upper middle class income strata who could otherwise afford and would be interested in private insurance coverage. Moreover, because it is the inevitable nature of government entitlement programs to have more static and restrictive designs (owing to bureaucratic and legislative rigidities and budget constraints), the crowd-out effect causes a limit to the utilization of existing and future innovative and flexible designs found in private LTCI (for example, equal access to home care as to institutional care). Finally, there does seem to be some public resentment to the spend-down rules in Medicaid as well as some public confusion about what Medicare and Medicaid cover in the LTSS area (leading to a lack of long-range personal financial planning), all of which would be obviated by more widespread use of private LTCI.
Proposal: A fraction (initially 75 percent, declining gradually over time) of the expected actuarial present value of Medicaid benefits by income level would be provided as a subsidy from the government (federal and state equally) to individuals at the point in time of claiming Social Security retirement benefits to purchase adequate permanent private long-term care insurance, including through combination policies. The standards for adequacy would include benefit levels sufficient to pay for average costs of home and institutional care in the current region of residence, lifetime benefits, and exclusion periods no greater than a year. "Permanent" means that the LTCI would have to be structured so that no lapses were allowed, such as through single-premium LTCI, the life care annuity, or similar products. Consistent with current law, the subsidy would decline as individual income (measured by the Social Security AIME) increased so that it would be large at the lowest income levels and would be eliminated at the very top of the income bands. It is anticipated that

financial planning software packages and financial planner advice would quickly recognize this major change in public policy and lead to the incremental expected lump-sum cost of LTCI at retirement to be included in household retirement planning and the setting of savings goals, likely causing a boost in lifetime savings rates. Finally, the resulting increase in total (public and private) resources from this proposal would put upward pressure on LTSS worker compensation and demand for enhanced qualifications.

3. **Financing—Create a comprehensive, understandable, and affordable LTSS financing system with both public and private components that work together effectively to enable individuals to plan for their LTSS needs.**

   Such a system would include the following components:
   - A public insurance program to broadly spread risk and help individuals pay for LTSS;
   - Expansion of private savings incentives and access to workplace savings options;
   - Reforms and improvements in the private long-term care insurance market including:
     - Providing greater standardization of private long-term care insurance policies while promoting innovations that benefit consumers;
     - Strengthening and updating consumer protections for tax-qualified policies;
     - Improving consumer information about these products; and
     - Examining opportunities to make the selection of long-term care insurance available when consumers make decisions about insurance or other benefits.
   - Information, educational resources, and/or tools for individuals to help them understand different financing options and make the choices that are best for them and their families.

Private Savings

4. **Increase substantially the amount of long-term care insurance/private savings/personal investments available to fund LTSS.** The populations needing LTSS are now using, and will in the future require, increasingly large amounts of federal and state funds at a time when the budgets of those governmental entities need to constrain rather than escalate their expenditures (see William

Hoagland testimony 6–27–13). The projected expenditures are unsustainable and can only be counteracted by immediate and prolonged efforts to change the LTSS funding system. On an individual level, it is vital that the public anticipate its potential future need for LTSS by purchasing long-term care insurance or by employing other financial savings vehicles. On a macro level, it is crucial to safeguard public budgets by ensuring that non-public dollars are available for injection into the LTSS funding stream.

Reasonable people can disagree as to whether the sources of personal funds should be long-term care insurance, annuities, pensions, personal savings, HSAs, retirement accounts, or some combination thereof, but federal regulations restricting the use of all these resources for funding LTSS should be relaxed or eliminated (see Lane Kent 8–1–13 testimony). Subsidies for the purchase of LTCI, if retained, should be redirected to middle-income and middle-age population, as agents selling LTCI indicate that persons with income in the $40,000–$50,000 range are good starter prospects. Educational campaigns should be introduced to create public awareness of the need to plan ahead for personal or family disability needs. As witnesses have testified, products and their marketing should be improved, including encouraging employers to offer family LTCI. AARP data show that U.S. businesses lose up to $33.6 billion per year in productivity from full-time caregiving employees and were found to be paying about 8 percent more for the health care of employees with elder care responsibilities.

5. **Amend Section 529 of the IRS code as called for in the Achieving a Better Life Experience Act of 2013 (ABLE Act; S. 313, H.R. 647) to address the unique needs of families with individuals with disabilities, particularly those waiting for Medicaid home and community-based services:** Across the country, an estimated 400,000 individuals are on waiting lists to receive long-term services and supports (LTSS); many of whom are children who will require these supports over their lifetime.[95] The ABLE Act will allow families of these children an opportunity to save for their needs. Currently, families are providing the bulk of their LTSS needs that in many cases comes at a significant cost to their ability to maintain and improve their economic circumstances, especially for the middle class.[96] AARP estimates that the economic impact of family caregiving for members with significant disabilities at $350 to $450 million per year. The

ABLE Act encourages work, savings, and asset development for families and individuals with disabilities that reduces dependence on scarce public benefits.

The ABLE Act allows families to set funds aside in a tax-advantaged savings account (ABLE accounts) that allows the funds to be withdrawn to cover qualified disability expenses such as health care, employment support, housing, transportation, assistive technology, and education. ABLE Accounts would amend and follow the existing Section 529 of the Internal Revenue Code for Qualified Tuition Programs so that they would be consistent with all the requirements and regulations of a traditional 529 qualified tuition program; they are easy to open and available in any state, and families can make the same annual contributions and enjoy the same tax-free treatment as under 529 accounts.[97] In this respect, ABLE accounts mirror a familiar and popular financial mechanism for many families.

The ABLE Act has broad bicameral and bipartisan support: S.313 was introduced by Sen. Robert Casey (D–PA) with 36 bipartisan cosponsors with 27 Democrats and 9 Republicans, and H.R. 647, introduced by Rep. Ander Crenshaw (R–FL–4), has 223 bipartisan cosponsors with 113 Democrats and 110 Republicans.

6. **Perform a well-designed analysis of private sources of funding** for long-term care supports and services and encourage implementation to provide private capital support for long-term care.
   a. Insurance products
      i. Encourage the development of simplified hybrid-type products (Life Care Annuity type approach).
      ii. Assess and expand if possible the conversion of life insurance policies to long-term care benefit plans.
      iii. Support/standardize LTC programs as components or options of Medicare Advantage.

b. Alternative Funding Sources/Incentives
   i. Allow tax-exempt and penalty-free distributions from qualified retirement plans to fund costs, programs, or premiums designed to provide long-term care.
   ii. Lift or remove Health Savings Account contribution cap.
   iii. Provide 529-type programs for long-term care.
      1. Possible support from payroll deductions.

iv. Develop insurance programs that insure for a limited front-end part of service delivery in order to enable more efficient and controlled use of public dollars.

Private LTC Insurance

7. **Education—Educational campaigns are needed to increase take-up of private long-term care insurance.** Surveys show that few people know they are at risk; they don't know that Medicare does not cover long-term care expenses and that people must be poor or divest themselves of their assets to qualify for Medicaid. Medicare, Medicaid, and Social Security are projected to consume half of all federal spending a decade from now. There is simply no money for new public programs to fill the gap between the millions of people needing care and the few prepared today to finance that care. Educating the public about these realities is crucial, as is providing options and incentives for them to purchase affordable, portable, reliable insurance.
8. **Education and other initiatives.**
   - Education campaign to clarify guidance on what the public programs (Medicare/Medicaid) provide and encourage early planning for retirement and LTSS needs.
   - Clarify FDA regulations to encourage the development of assistive care technology.
   - Encourage small business investment through SBIR, STTR, and SBA to develop assistive technology.
   - Recommend to Office of the National Coordinator for Health Information Technology to provide, as part of implementing "meaningful use" Stage 3 standards, an optional place for recording care plans in the electronic health record.
9. **There is a strong need to encourage the development of personal and family capacity—through private insurance, savings, and otherwise—for their retirement and LTSS expenses.**

   A. Long-Term Care Insurance
      - As is the case with Medigap insurance, establish federal standards to standardize and simplify the types of policies insurers can offer in order to facilitate comparison and competition.
      - HHS, in cooperation with the states, creates an electronic market and provides information and direct assistance to

consumers in order to facilitate comparison shopping and educated choices.
   - Relieve state regulations on high-deductible, long-term care insurance products, thereby providing for catastrophic insurance coverage and for clarity to families about the amount they need to save for LTSS deductibles or provide for in their Medigap policies.
   - Working with the states, HHS calls for the establishment of reinsurance arrangements, financed by private insurers that establish parameters for risk management and mitigate risks to individual companies.
   - Allow above-the-line tax deductions for long-term care insurance premiums.
   - Exclude value of long-term insurance policies or payments from Medicaid eligibility requirements.

B. Private Savings

- Allow tax-exempt, penalty-free withdrawal from qualified retirement funds to fund LTC insurance or LTSS expenses.
  - 401K
  - 402B
  - IRA
  - Roth IRA
- Amend Section 125 plans (cafeteria) to include LTC insurance.
- Lift or remove Health Savings Account (HSA) contribution cap.
- Amend IRC to establish tax-exempt ABLE accounts to assist an individual and families with an actual or anticipated disability in building an account to pay for qualified disability expenses, including long-term care insurance premiums (see, e.g., Introduced as S. 313, H.R. 647).

10. **Create new federal regulations allowing the private insurance sector** (i.e., health, long-term care, disability, and/or life) **to create a new generation of simple, easy-to-understand, affordable, and standardized insurance products targeted for purchase by working individuals.** These products should be marketed through employers and could be offered as a supplemental benefit at the employer's discretion. These products should also be backed by state/regional reinsurance pools to ensure greater affordability.
11. **Protect consumers from inappropriate denials of coverage from any public or private LTSS financing system.**

a. Develop enforceable national consumer protections for all private longterm care insurance models.
b. Provide consumer-friendly, meaningful appeals in all public and private financing systems.

12. **Allow the life care annuity to be used as an investment in tax-advantaged retirement accounts.** Motivation: The life care annuity is a combination insurance product innovation that reduces adverse selection in its immediate life annuity portion, resulting in lower premiums, and would allow for a considerable relaxation of underwriting standards for its long-term care insurance portion. Common purchase of this product would accommodate the delayed purchase of LTCI until closer to retirement, reducing various pricing risks on the insurer, while at same time providing permanent coverage (that is, not subject to the risk of lapses) to the insured. Under current law, it is not allowed to be used as an investment or distribution mechanism in employer-sponsored retirement plans or in retirement accounts such as IRAs, unless taken as a taxable distribution.

    Proposal: Allowing the life care annuity to be used as an investment in tax-advantaged retirement accounts would essentially give the LTCI portion tax-favored status equivalent to the tax deductibility of premiums. But in the form of the life care annuity, it would be tied to other desirable public policy goals—permanent LTCI coverage, and improvement in the efficiency of life annuity markets. Technical tax requirements governing retirement assets such as minimum distribution requirements and incidental benefit rules would be waived for the LTCI portion of the life care annuity.

13. **Lighten regulatory burdens on private LTCI.** Motivation: A significant part of the current difficulties for writers of LTCI lies in the regulatory inflexibilities of the product to respond to rapid and large changes in the macroeconomic environment, especially with regard to interest and inflation rates. In particular, the recent rapid and sustained drops in interest rates induced by unusual Federal Reserve monetary policies, as well as the drop in inflation rates caused by the Great Recession, have made LTCI unprofitable to writers (because it was priced assuming much higher investment returns) and expensive to consumers (because the requirement for automatic annual 5% increases in benefits in tax-qualified LTCI implicitly assumes a more inflationary environment).

Proposal: For sufficiently large changes in the macroeconomic environment, allow (in the upward direction) and require (in the downward direction) writers of LTCI to change automatically the pricing of existing outstanding LTCI policies on an actuarially fair basis; the same would apply to the requirement for inflation adjustment in benefits. The "sufficiently large" nature of the macroeconomic changes would be determined by the National Association of Insurance Commissioners on a uniform national basis. All other desired pricing and product changes arising from other sources of actuarial experience, such as claims and lapses, and so on, which are generally more specific to the business judgment and actuarial skill of the insurer, would continue to be governed by current state laws requiring specific state commissioner approvals of pricing and product changes.

14. **Regulatory Reform for LTCI.** Currently, long-term care insurance products often suffer from a lack of portability. For instance, an individual who purchases an LTC insurance policy while living and working in New York and subsequently moves to Florida upon retirement may find difficulty accessing benefits after moving to a new state. This lack of portability discourages take-up of private LTC policies, increasing the burden on public programs in the process.

    One possible solution to this problem could involve the formation of multistate compacts to ensure portability of LTC policies for all states participating in the compact. The National Association of Insurance Commissioners (NAIC) could help to develop such a system, which would allow states themselves to suggest the best possible solutions, rather than having a top-down model imposed by Washington. To the extent that federal policymakers wish to support the NAIC endeavor, a gain-sharing demonstration—in which any potential reductions in public expenditures arising from the compact are shared with the states participating in it—would both encourage states to participate and promote a new regulatory framework designed to alleviate the burdens on the public purse.

15. **Tax Incentives.** As was noted in testimony at the most recent commission hearing, the federal government provides significant tax incentives to encourage participation in both health care and retirement programs. Incentives for employer-provided health insurance and for contributions to pension and 401(k) plans represent some of the largest incentives in the tax code. Yet the incentives to

purchase private long-term care insurance are small by comparison, particularly given that private insurance can alleviate the financial burdens placed on Medicare and Medicaid as the Baby Boomers retire.

The obvious solution to this problem would involve equalizing the tax treatment of health insurance and long-term care insurance by allowing LTC insurance premiums to be paid through a Section 125 cafeteria plan. Other similar solutions would allow for taxand penalty-free distributions from retirement savings accounts like IRAs and 401(k)s, and the use of LTC policies in life care annuities without triggering taxable distributions.

Equalizing the tax treatment between health and long-term care insurance would effectively provide a 30–40% discount on current LTC premiums. Moreover, by encouraging broader take-up of private policies, such incentives could reduce both adverse selection and administrative loading—thereby lowering premiums further.

Secondarily, equalizing the tax treatment of health insurance and longterm care insurance could encourage the introduction of hybrid health/longterm care insurance products—a solution presented by one of our panelists last week. In the absence of equal treatment for both products, the tax complexities presented by hybrid policies could serve as a major disincentive to their widespread adoption.

16. **Tax incentives.** All levels of government are facing serious budget constraints that threaten funding for existing health care, disability, and retirement programs. To assure that the safety net is secure for the most vulnerable in our society, we need to provide new incentives for those who can prepare now to take responsibility for their own long-term care needs. However, sales of individual long-term care insurance policies have been declining for a decade, and fewer and fewer companies are selling the policies. The share of the market represented by people aged 40–69 in middleand lower-income categories is declining. We need new incentives, new partnerships, and innovative programs to address these challenges.

    Recommendation: Equalize the tax treatment of health insurance and longterm care insurance. As a first step, this could include allowing employees to use pre-tax dollars through Section 125 "cafeteria" plans and/or through Flexible Spending Accounts to purchase long-term care insurance. States could also provide tax credits, as Minnesota has done with its $100-a-year credit for those who enroll in long-term care insurance.

Changing the tax treatment of long-term care insurance would incentivize creation of a more robust market for these products. Witness Jason Brown described an integrated insurance product consisting of a life annuity policy combined with long-term care insurance, offering evidence that this could be a stable market even if the product were purchased at or near retirement. Our Vice Chair, Mark Warshawsky, has produced a detailed plan describing this innovative solution, "The Life Care Annuity: A Proposal for an Insurance Product Innovation to Simultaneously Improve Financing and Benefit Provision for Long-Term Care and to Insure the Risk of Outliving Assets in Retirement."

This is not a solution for everyone but is for those who can afford to begin planning for their own future needs. Adding new incentives for people to purchase private insurance protection and reduce the disincentives for people to begin preparing for their own needs will mean the public safety net will be stronger for the most vulnerable who have no other alternatives and must rely on public support to finance their care. We received public testimony from Rebecca Underwood, parent/guardian/advocate for Aaron Underwood, to explain so very clearly how important it is to make sure the resources are available for those with the most critical needs.

17. **Site-Neutral Payments should produce notable savings; a portion of the savings would be tax rebates for LTSS, and a portion would be used as subsidies for low-income individuals.** As discussed above, many believe that a site-neutral payment system would produce savings and achieve better outcomes for patients. In an effort to improve quality of care and generate cost-saving concepts, a new patient-focused payment model would be developed that would reduce spending on post-acute care while facilitating movement toward a more rational system for PAC payment and delivery. This model would focus on the needs of the patients rather than the setting of care, with the potential to reduce federal spending approximately $15–20 billion over the 10-year budget window.

    The savings from such an initiative could be used to create tax rebates for LTSS use or purchase of an LTSS private financing option, such as Private LTSS Insurance. Additionally, a portion of such savings could be used to create a subsidy program for those with low income to purchase private LTSS options.

Medicare Eligibility and Benefits

18. **Create new regulations and accountability standards for a new generation of Medicare Advantage/Special Needs Plans and/or Medigap coverage** that would cover specified long-term care services as an optional supplemental benefit. To ensure proper evaluation of the financing models needed to sustain these new models, updating the CMS Hierarchical Condition Categories to better reflect the clinical and functional profile of high-risk, high-utilizing beneficiaries should be required.
19. **Make the most of Medicare—the one national program we have now by removing current barriers to Medicare coverage for people with long-term and chronic conditions.**
    1. Redefine the homebound requirement for Medicare home health coverage so that people who cannot obtain the services they need outside the home can obtain them at home.
        a. Currently the homebound definition restricts some people from getting care at home although they cannot consistently leave home to obtain the services they need.
        b. Do NOT add a cap or co-insurance to the Medicare home health benefit.
            i. Proposals are being considered to limit home care, which would further exacerbate the already limited ability of people to obtain home and community-based services.
            ii. The savings estimate, at $730 million/10years for the co-pay, does not warrant this further limitation on home care.
    2. Remove the three-day hospital stay requirement for skilled nursing facility (SNF) coverage so people without the need for an acute inpatient hospital stay can at least get some Medicare nursing facility coverage.
        i. Absent removing the three-day requirement, eliminate hospital "observation status," or count all days spent in the hospital as "inpatient" for purposes of qualifying for subsequent SNF stays.

3. Eliminate the 24-month Medicare eligibility waiting period for people who qualify for Social Security Disability Insurance (SSDI).
4. Ensure the *Jimmo* v. *Sebelius* settlement is effectively implemented to eliminate the "improvement standard" requirement for determining Medicare coverage and ensure coverage is also available for skilled services to maintain an individual's condition or slow deterioration.

20. **Add a new Long-Term Services and Support (LTSS) benefit to Medicare.** The LTSS benefit would be triggered when an individual is certified to be dependent in two or more activities of daily living and/or has cognitive or mental health issues such that independence is contraindicated. In such cases the individual would be eligible for:
   a. Skilled nursing facility coverage for up to 150 days per calendar year;
      i. Without the need for a three-day hospital stay;
      ii. Without the need for daily skilled care (custodial care alone would be covered).
   b. Home health coverage, including coverage for home health aide services, without the need for a skilled service;
   c. Personal care attendant;
   d. Care management and coordination;
   e. Adult day center;
   f. Respite care to support family or other volunteer caregiver;
   g. Outpatient therapy without an annual cap;
   h. Other reasonable and necessary services.

   Note: The CLASS Act experience demonstrates that any such LTSS benefit must be mandatory in order to be financially viable.

- Various options are possible, but a new Medicare LTSS benefit should not add to the complexity of Medicare and should not diminish the stability of the current program.
- Consider adding the LTSS benefit to Medicare Part A, with a defined % increase to current Part A payroll tax to pay for it. This additional may even strengthen Medicare Part A, which is mandatory for those with Medicare.

Medicaid Eligibility and Benefits

21. **Create a national Medicaid Buy-In (MBI) program for workers with significant disabilities up to 250% of FPL.** Medicaid is the only affordable option to access long-term services and supports for millions of people with significant disabilities. Standard health insurance policies do not offer coverage for the long-term services and supports (LTSS) required for individuals with disabilities to live in the community. And although private long-term care insurance coverage does exist, it is not a realistic option for working-age individuals with disabilities. To help provide access to affordable LTSS to working people with disabilities, Congress gave states an option to let working individuals with disabilities continue to receive LTSS through the Medicaid program when their income or resources exceed Medicaid's normal limits through an option known as the Medicaid Buy-In, or MBI, programs. States can implement MBI programs under two different authorities: the Balanced Budget Act of 1997 or the Ticket to Work & Work Incentives Improvement Act of 1999. Forty-six states currently have MBI programs, and more than 200,000 workers with disabilities are currently working and receiving needed LTSS as result of this option. The different authorities impose different requirements states must follow in creating MBI programs:

	Balanced Budget Act	***Ticket to Work***
Age limits	None	16-64
Income Limits	Up to 250% of FPL	None
Resource Limits	Up to state	Up to state
Premiums	Based on sliding scale – no upper limit	Premiums and cost sharing based on income
Definition of work	States cannot define work	States cannot define work
Grace period for employment	Limited	Not allowed

Although MBI programs offer opportunities for people with disabilities who work to continue to receive LTSS, the variation in state programs and some design flaws limit the effectiveness of these programs to support working individuals with disabilities—forcing people not to take promotions to remain within income or resource limits; making it difficult, if not impossible to relocate for a better position; and making people less likely to work because of not being able to get back onto regular Medicaid if their work attempt fails.

The program would have no upper age limit, with a standard definition of work, grace periods for unemployment that recognize the episodic nature of many disabilities, allow people to save for current and future needs and retirement, and disregard resources accumulated during MBI participation for access to Medicaid if a person can no longer work. Here are some specifics:

- Income limits vary from a low of 80% of FPL to unlimited income;
- Resource limits vary from a low of regular Medicaid limits ($2000 for an individual) up to unlimited resources;
- No grace period for participation;
- No pathway back to regular Medicaid if a person accumulated resources while participating in MBI; and
- Uncertainty regarding eligibility for Medicaid at age 65.

22. **Pilot a program for workers with significant disabilities whose earnings exceed 250% FPL and need LTSS to remain employed without support from the Social Security income assistance programs.** *U.S. Disability Support Systems Fail People With Disabilities:* The United States has made significant strides in changing the expectations of and attitudes toward people with disabilities. The passage of landmark civil rights legislation in the Americans with Disabilities Act (ADA) in 1990 contributed to this evolution of attitudes and creation of opportunities. Court decisions, such as the Supreme Court decision in the historic Olmstead case, have also called for the full integration of individuals with disabilities in society. And while many doors have been opened, the lack of pathways to access needed services and supports that allow people with significant disabilities to live and work independently while achieving even a modest level of economic security has hindered the progress that might otherwise have been made.

    Individuals with Disabilities Face Unique Challenges: People with significant disabilities who require supports and services to work often face a catch–22. Currently, Medicaid is the only option available that provides access to the services and supports needed to get and keep a job. Private long-term care insurance is not an option for a variety of reasons, including: denial of coverage outright; cost-prohibitive premiums if one is able to get coverage; services and supports not available in a work setting; and/or a short timeframe of authorized benefits. Self-financing the services and supports is out of the question for all but the highest earners and makes people with disabilities less economically competitive than their non-disabled peers. And although many working people have access to private health insurance, and more will gain it through the Affordable Care Act, private health insurance does not cover at all or inadequately covers many needed services and supports.

Medicaid, While Vital, Doesn't Work for Many Working People with Disabilities: Although Medicaid is the only game in town, it is also an imperfect solution. Medicaid is intended to provide health care and related long-term services and supports to individuals with limited income (both earned and unearned) and resources. Medicaid work incentives allow working people with disabilities to continue their participation in the Medicaid program while allowing them to increase their earnings up to a set limit (usually 250% of FPL) and, in some very limited cases, save for emergency expenses or life goals. These work incentives include, but are not limited to, the Medicaid Buy-In programs and the 1619(b) program.[98] However, as Medicaid was designed to provide healthcare to low-income individuals with no other access to insurance coverage, its structure and eligibility rules make it difficult to impossible for working individuals with significant disabilities to achieve the things associated with a middle-class lifestyle for a number of reasons.

- Upper limits on income and resources for program eligibility are often the drivers of career decisions rather than opportunities.
- Variations in state Medicaid programs (e.g., income and resource limits for MBI participation, income limits for eligibility, types of waivers and whether slots are available, and the package of services and supports available) make relocating for a better opportunity difficult, if not impossible.
- SSI/Medicaid's resource limits (e.g., a person can have no more than $2,000 in assets for an individual or $3,000 for a couple to be Medicaid eligible) are often problematic, making it impossible for people with disabilities who work to save for emergencies and retirement, let alone save to purchase a home or start a business.
- People with significant disabilities often have extraordinary support needs that make it difficult, if not impossible, to get those needs met outside of public programs.

- People with disabilities often find themselves in the unenviable position of turning down jobs or promotions to maintain access to these vital services and supports. The U.S. must provide people with disabilities a pathway to access service and supports that allows them to earn to their potential, save for their futures, achieve a middle-class lifestyle, and achieve the vision of the ADA.

Proposal: A pilot program that provides access to the services and supports needed by employed individuals with significant disabilities (meet SSA definition of disability absent the inability to work assessment) combined with a waiver of rules that prevent people with disabilities to earn income and accumulate assets without jeopardizing access to services and supports. This program is designed to wrap around health insurance products (offered by employer or through the state marketplaces) and modeled on the 1619(b) program; specific program design elements include:

- Eligibility: To be eligible to receive wrap-around services and supports through this program, a person would have to be a working individual with a disability defined as:
  - Meeting or equaling the Social Security disability listings or qualifying for quick disability determination/compassionate allowances for eligibility for the Social Security disability programs.
  - Be working, defined as earnings at or above 250% FPL.
- Pay applicable cost sharing based on income, employment-related disability expenses, as well as level of services needed.
- Wrap-around package: The program would offer access to services and supports that people with disabilities need to become and stay employed and fill coverage gaps between what is offered by health care insurance products and the unique health care needs of individuals with significant disabilities. The services and supports package available through the program would include: personal attendant care, assistive technology, and other services and supports.

23. **Tighten Medicaid eligibility for people age 62 and older by considering assets currently excluded from eligibility tests as countable and by removing opportunities for gaming program rules.** Motivation: Given severe state and federal government budget constraints and the concomitant tendency for the government to cut

Medicaid reimbursements to providers, thereby harming quality, public resources need to be focused on providing care to the needy and poor, not the upper middle class and the well-to-do households to enable them to leave large bequests.

Proposals: Limit the home equity exemption to $50,000 (this would redirect many households to use reverse mortgages to fund LTSS and discourage the game of investing otherwise countable assets in exempt homes). Extend the look-back period for real estate to 10 years, as it is administratively easy to accomplish. Outlaw Medicaid-friendly, fixed-period annuities and Miller trusts, currently used as eligibility gaming devices. Include retirement assets (401(k) accounts, IRAs, etc.) in countable assets unless they are being distributed as an immediate straight life (not fixed-period) annuity, whereby they would be included as countable income. Include premiums being paid for life insurance as countable income. Any assets that are exempted and not divested should be available for estate recovery by the states, which activity needs to be aggressively overseen and enforced by the federal government.

B. Service Delivery Ideas

Strengthen Medicaid

1. **Medicaid—Strengthen and maintain Medicaid as a safety net that effectively targets and utilizes resources, leverages technology, encourages innovation, rewards quality, and honors consumers' choice of and access to the services and supports they need in the setting of their preference by:**
   - Requiring coverage of HCBS for eligible individuals, just as for institutional care;
     - In the short term, providing financial incentives to build state and local capacity to make the transition to HCBS as the primary LTSS system;
   - Enabling consumers and their spouses to stay in their homes and communities by increasing the Medicaid asset test and indexing it to inflation and by making permanent spousal impoverishment protections for HCBS, consistent with such protections for the spouses of nursing home residents;

- Urging states that choose to implement Medicaid-managed LTSS to use these programs to balance resources so more beneficiaries and their families can receive HCBS;
- Requiring states that use Medicaid-managed LTSS to provide important consumer protections including: promoting consumer choices, creating adequate networks to assure access to services, administering strong oversight to assure quality, and measuring outcomes such as consumer experience;
- Offering consumers the option of self-direction, including allowing for the payment of family caregivers to provide services, as in the successful Cash and Counseling Demonstration; and
- Provide incentives for innovative, high-quality residential settings, including those licensed as nursing homes, like Green Houses, and those licensed as assisted living or other models of housing and services.

Rebalance LTSS

2. **Eliminate the institutional bias in Medicaid LTSS**. Barrierand regulation-free selection and choice of location to receive LTSS would allow substantial numbers of Medicaid-eligible clients to remain at or to return home at lower cost than living in institutional facilities. In her 8–1–13 testimony, Patti Killingsworth goes further by recommending that HCBS be the default selection. Killingsworth also suggests mandating individual cost neutrality as another mechanism for creating economies in the program. While critics express concern about the "woodwork effect," a number of studies would indicate otherwise. More evidence-based programming is also important. Insufficient effort has been devoted to research that would demonstrate the most careand cost-effective LTSS needed to allow someone to remain safely at home.

   In relation to person-centered care, the rigidity of Medicaid regulations often hinders or obstructs the selection and delivery of the most appropriate care for individual clients and their informal caregivers. Consideration should be given to review of regulations and statutes that thwart the goal of providing proper care. The Older Americans Act (OAA) offers the type of flexibility that should be used as a model for providing services. It is attuned with individual and local needs, brings community resources into the system, and administratively is far less costly than Medicaid.

3. **Rebalance Medicaid Long-Term Services and Supports (LTSS).** The vast majority of Medicaid beneficiaries of any age who require LTSS prefer to receive those services in their own home or in a community-based setting instead of living in an institution—known as home and community-based services (HCBS). As a whole, the United States still over relies on the institutional side of LTSS. Despite the increase from 2.1 to 3.2 million HCBS users since 2000, states still only spend 36.8% of their LTSS budgets on HCBS for aging and physical disability populations. The range varies widely with the highest performing state spending 62% on HCBS and the lowest 10%. Only seven states spend more than 50% on HCBS (AARP 2011 Scorecard).

   Nursing home utilization also varies widely across the states, with 838 persons per 100,000 of state population occupying NF beds in the highest state to 84 in the lowest.

   On the Developmental Disability side, only Mississippi spends less than 50% on HCBS. But of 4.9 million persons with developmental disabilities nationwide, 4.1 million live with their families, of which it is estimated that 25% of the caregivers or parents are over age 60. And many persons with developmental disabilities languish on long waiting lists (two-thirds of 511,174 individuals that 38 states report on HCBS waiting lists) (from the Kaiser 2012 data update).

   Currently many state Medicaid programs are consumed by exploring ways to expand health care to low-income populations or to more efficiently serve already covered populations. The capacity of these agencies to simultaneously overhaul and maximize the efficiency of their LTSS systems is under considerable strain. Partly for this reason, many states are looking to managed care organizations to administer their Medicaid LTSS systems.

   Proposal: This proposal would create a single HCBS state plan authority that unifies and bundles the best features of the options described above and would make permanent the enhanced match incentives in the Money Follows the Person (MFP) program and the Balancing Incentive Program (BIP). The key features would include:

   - States can set needs-based functional eligibility less stringent than the institutional level of care (LOC).
   - Allows states to include any or all Medicaid eligibility groups with income standards up to 300% of SSI, with strategies

incorporated to ensure the lowest-income individuals receive coverage first.

- Allows states to craft multiple programs or consolidate multiple programs across disability or other target groups in a manner that adheres to applicable laws (ADA, etc.).
- Payments for HCBS services are 6% higher than the regular match rate, subject to Secretarial approval, using criteria reflective of autonomy, choice, and applicable rules related to HCBS characteristics. The Secretary will determine the specific HCBS services, settings, and attributes that will be eligible for the enhanced FFP, including time periods for review of enhanced FMAP eligibility.
- Institutional services are held at the regular match rate.
- Makes permanent the MFP feature of full FFP for HCBS costs for one year after relocation from a nursing home, hospital, ICF/DD, or PRTF where a person has resided for more than 90 days and includes features of both MFP and the "K" to pay for certain start-up costs.
- Adds Partial Residential Treatment facilities (PRTF) as an allowable alternative for LOC determinations.
- As a state plan option, states must serve all eligible individuals; however, a state may negotiate enrollment growth targets tied to specific rebalancing benchmarks that permanently decrease the state's institutional footprint.
- Allows a time-limited differential match for buy down of vacant institutional beds taken offline.
- Allows a state under this authority to create health homes to coordinate care for a subset of eligible individuals who are receiving HCBS services and have two or more chronic conditions, and the state can receive 90% FMAP for up to eight quarters as defined in the Affordable Care Act.
- Includes opportunities for easy linkage to tools for integration, such as health homes and managed care authorities, setting forth uniform expectations yet streamlined authority linkage quality and reporting structures.
- Will create the possibility for a medically needy income level for community-based services.

The single-state HCBS authority would also have uniform requirements including:

- Meets HCBS settings requirements;
- Needs assessments include core elements for all populations but also address specific populations using valid and reliable population-specific assessments;
- Person-centered planning requirements for all participants;
- No Wrong Door for all intake and eligibility;
- Requires a mitigation plan for potential conflicts of interests in the delivery of case management; and
- Participant direction, including hiring and firing authority over personal care staff and access to an individual budget must be an available option.

Specified Quality Measures

The provision will also "clean up" the statute to remove the various provisions (driftwood) to definitively provide a sleek option. However, states may still elect to utilize the 1915(c) authority to fund HCBS services tied to an institutional level of care, subject to the periodic review by the Secretary to ensure that the services offered therein comport with established standards for HCBS.

4. **Removing the Institutional Bias.** Medicaid's bias towards institutional, as opposed to home and community-based care, stems in part from its original design, and in part from budgetary strictures that have impeded the road to reform in the years since. Traditionally, the Congressional Budget Office has stated that expanding HCBS could cost more money than it saves—largely due to a potential "woodwork effect" caused when family caregivers utilize expanded access to Medicaid's HCBS services.

   However, testimony last week provided several potential ways to alleviate the budgetary impact of any "woodwork effect" as a result of a transition from institutional care to HCBS. Specifically, Tennessee's recommendations to make institutional care an optional benefit, mandate cost-neutrality for HCBS, require beneficiaries to "opt-in" to institutional care, and require enrollment in HCBS first prior to placement in an institution all would tilt the bias away from institutional and towards community-based care. These reforms could also provide "scoreable" budgetary savings that would reduce any increased spending from a potential "woodwork effect"—a critical consideration, given the current fiscal climate.

As one panel noted last week, removing the institutional bias in Medicaid cannot be achieved overnight. However, the recommendations provided could represent important ways to provide better care to more beneficiaries, at the same or lower cost—a true "win-win" solution.

5. **Rebalance Medicaid so that institutional bias is removed**, and people who qualify for Medicaid can obtain necessary LTSS in the least restrictive setting that meets their needs.
6. **Remove "institutional bias".** Payment policies in current programs for LTSS make it more difficult for people to get care in alternative settings, including receiving care at home or other residential settings. We have heard testimony from witnesses describing the possibilities of new technologies and delivery systems that can improve care and save unnecessary spending. Allowing greater access to HCBC is the obvious solution, but it must be structured in such a way that it doesn't create a woodwork effect. Marilyn Moon in her testimony suggested replacing the three-day hospitalization requirement for eligibility for skilled nursing care with "a more needs-based approach . . . Specific criteria concerning the need for SNF care should be the determining factor, not an arbitrary rule." Witness Patti Killingsworth suggested an "opt-in" approach to institutional care and that enrollment in HCBC be required before placement in an institution—a kind of "step therapy" for nursing care.
7. **Rebalance the current national health care system, oriented toward acute care and safety net programs, to increase Home and Community-Based Care.** Doing so will require three changes: (1) Alter the design of Medicaid to focus on home and community-based and eliminate its "institutional bias" and at the same time achieve greater consistency across the states in their approach to HCBS, (2) provide greater flexibility to the States in the administration of their Medicaid programs subject to clear federal performance and quality standards, supporting states with the technical and administrative support needed to reorient their programs to include more home and community-based elements, and (3) introducing into Medicare a care-coordinated, caregiver-centric support program to strengthen the capacity of American families to support home and community-based care.

A. Medicaid

- Require states to offer community and home-based care option with determination to be made on basis of functional impairment.
- Provide consistent information on availability of services, both institutional as well as home and community based, regardless of your point of entry into care and require the use of a universal assessment tool to evaluate need and placement.
- Decouple eligibility for HCBS from a determination of nursing home eligibility.
- Consolidate and simplify waivers to states with performance-based requirements and gain-sharing.
- Provide states with technical and administrative support to encourage move to HCBS and to build the needed community infrastructure to support HCBS.
- Develop standard quality measures for both home as well as institutional LTC facilities.

B. Medicare

- Provide a new caregiver support benefit for Medicare eligibles with functional impairments in order to support more HCBS. (Need to determine basis of eligibility and cost.)
- Replace three-day prior hospitalization requirement with a need assessment-based approach designed to encourage post-acute HCBS.
- Require and reimburse physicians as part of annual wellness visit to prepare a care plan for each beneficiary (researching recent regulation to determine if necessary).
- Direct the ONC to work with the Agency for Health Research and Quality and Centers for Medicare and Medicaid Services in plan standardizing some elements of the care planning process, the care plan documentation, the continuity of care plans across settings of care, and the evaluation of the performance of care plans.

Care Integration/Care Management—Duals

8. **System Transformation and Care Coordination**—Create a more responsive, efficient, and integrated LTSS delivery system that ensures that people can access quality services in settings that they choose by:

- Establishing a more effective system to measure and reward quality, including:
  - Developing and implementing better measures of quality of life and care that are tested and validated across settings (especially in HCBS) by a consensus body;
  - Rewarding quality care based on validated measures that have been tested by pilot projects in various settings; and
  - Establishing systems to publicly report quality and cost that will be understandable to consumers as they compare providers and plans and make decisions about services.
- Using technology more effectively to mobilize and integrate community resources and to share information among providers, individuals, and family caregivers across settings, in order to:
  - Promote more effective integration with health care services, including extension of "meaningful use" incentives to LTSS providers as that becomes feasible;
  - Improve person-centered data collection to support the delivery of person-and family-centered care across settings

    and through transitions; Permit real-time monitoring and timely interventions to address quality problems; and
  - Support greater independence by mobilizing and coordinating local community services such as transportation, shopping, and home maintenance services.
- Align the incentives to improve the integration of health care and LTSS services in a person-centered approach rather than one tied to specific settings by:
  - Broadening the Center for Medicare and Medicaid Innovation's work to include more focus on the integration of LTSS with health care services;
  - Reforming payment systems to promote systems transformation; Including better data sharing between Medicare and Medicaid; and
  - Supporting partnerships among health care, post-acute, and LTSS providers.
- Creating livable communities that build on housing and services models to improve health care and LTSS coordination, and expand local initiatives, such as Villages, that coordinate

community services to enable people with disabilities to live more independently.
- Establishing a clear point of contact so that individuals and their family caregivers know who they can turn to when they need assistance, especially in transitions across settings.
- Incentivizing states to test and develop models that could potentially inform federal policy.

9. **Medicare payment/delivery reform innovation to target people needing long-term services and support.**
   Premise:
   - The 15% of Medicare beneficiaries with chronic conditions and functional impairments account for about a third of Medicare spending.
   - Fewer than half of these beneficiaries are Medicaid beneficiaries (dual eligibles).
   - The federal government finances 80 percent of Medicare and Medicaid spending on dual eligibles, predominantly through Medicare.
   - The federal government has a responsibility to promote better integrated care through Medicare, rather than shift responsibility to Medicaid.

   Proposal:
   The Centers for Medicare and Medicaid Services should use their authority to launch a Medicare payment and delivery reform pilot to promote provider initiatives that: (1) focus on people who need long-term services and supports, (2) coordinate services across the continuum to address long-term services and supports needs along with medical needs, and (3) work, in general, for all Medicare beneficiaries with long-term care needs, regardless of income or Medicaid eligibility. Such pilots would include: Monthly payments per enrolled patient to participating providers sufficient to support coordinators and other currently uncovered care management services; shared savings with providers who satisfy quality standards; provider accountability for savings sufficient to offset care coordination expenses; and shared savings with states that participate and invest in delivery improvement for dual eligibles.
10. **Further national and state efforts to fully integrate Medicare and Medicaid financing and service delivery for those who are dually eligible** in order to improve person-centered outcomes while lowering

costs. In particular, CMS should continue to focus on two goals: (a) development and implementation of quality measures and service monitoring across the entire continuum of care including HCBS, and (b) upholding strong consumer protections such as transparent three-way contracts, state and health plan readiness reviews, ombudsman programs, and mechanisms for seamless transitions and continuity of care.

11. **Improvement in the quality of care for dual eligibles.** A number of witnesses spoke to the need for better management and integration of care among providers, payers and patients. Among other problems, they noted the difficulties in maneuvering the publicly funded system, the fragmented relationship of dual eligibles to their health and LTSS funders, the difficulties in transitions between care settings, the complications in establishing provider relationships, and the struggles in determining appropriate patient care. Clearly the system needs major work to develop better client supports, improve care coordination, remove redundancies and gaps in the system, prevent unnecessary hospitalization and nursing home placement, and preserve funds. States are adopting a variety of models for dual-eligible clients. While bringing about both economies and improved quality of care, these programs allow for differences in state environments. Additionally, innovations that provide greater fungibility of resources, such as in Tennessee and Rhode Island, should be reviewed for replicability, quality of care, and overall cost. A much-needed overhaul in service can result in a far more efficient cost-effective system.

    Please note, as stated above, additions to publicly funded LTSS need to be **expenditure neutral.**

12. **Care Coordination:** The recent expansion of Medicaid-managed care for dual-eligible populations needing LTSS reflects the belief of many states that managed-care options can provide better coordination than the traditional state-run Medicaid model. Unfortunately, however, states looking to innovate in this sphere often face additional burdens imposed by Washington.

    Freeing states from these federal requirements could expand the utilization of Medicaid managed-care options, particularly for dual-eligible beneficiaries. Solutions in this vein would include allowing states to utilize one Medicaid managed-care organization in a given region if that region's population is too limited to support two organizations. Another possible reform could give states the option to incentivize beneficiaries who participate in healthy behaviors and disease prevention activities, or to offer additional services for those beneficiaries choosing high-value or managed care plans. These types of reforms would increase participation in coordinated care models, encouraging activities that lead to improved quality of care and thus reduced health expenditures.

13. **Coordinated care:** A recent study in the *Medicare and Medicaid Research Review* found that a "bundled hospital payment system that covers both acute and post-acute care can create financial incentives in the Medicare fee-forservice system to foster care coordination, improving the current disorganized system of post-acute care." Witness Barbara Gage stressed the need for eliminating care silos and suggested that ACOs establish programs to target high-risk populations and to then provide follow-up care through community-based organizations.

    The silo- and rule-driven approach to care delivery interferes with quality patient care and is a terrible waste of resources. We received public comment from, Carol Marshall, a health care consultant in Fort Worth, Texas, explaining the extraordinarily rigid rules involving payment policy for physical, occupational, and speech therapy that create stress for both medical professionals and patients, blocking the ability of practitioners to provide patient-centered care. Witness Patti Killingsworth also recommending realigning "incentives in the Medicare program to support delivery of Medicare and Medicaid LTSS in the most integrated setting possible," and she offered specific solutions to achieve that goal.

14. **Develop a national care-management system based on the Georgia Source Program:** Georgia maintains a program called Service Options Using Resources in a Community Environment, or SOURCE. The SOURCE program is unique to Georgia. It is a State Plan enhanced primary care case management program that serves frail elderly and disabled beneficiaries to improve the health outcomes of persons with chronic health conditions by linking primary medical care with home and community-based services.

    SOURCE links primary medical care and case management with approved long-term health services in a person's home or community to prevent hospital and nursing home care. All SOURCE clients must be eligible for Medicaid and meet nursing home level of care.

SOURCE serves aged, blind and disabled Georgians who are eligible for Supplemental Security Income/Medicaid (SSI). An assessment helps to determine how much care a participant needs. An individual care path is designed based on the need for medical monitoring and assistance with functional tasks. Family members and other informal caregivers as well as staff from support agencies participate in care paths. In addition to core services, SOURCE offers personal support services, assisted living services, extended home health, home-delivered meals, adult day health care, emergency response services, and 24-hour medical access to a case manager and primary care physician.

The proposal would take the original SOURCE model one step further and create a SOURCE Patient Centered Health Home Model (PCHH). The PCHH model would include the following additions:

- Expand SOURCE covered services to include some or all of the following:
  a. Skilled Nursing Facility (SNF)
  b. Home Health
  c. Hospice
  d. Physician
  e. Pharmacy

The PCHH model also includes six innovative elements to achieve the goals outlined above. These are:

- Care management which includes those receiving Skilled Nursing Facility care;
- Varying levels of care management based upon Resource Utilization Groups (RUGS) and case mix indices (CMI's) to reduce care gaps that can occur between levels of acuity and different service settings;
- A no wrong door access;
- An information technology solution to permit the support of data sharing in real time across the network and more closely link a comprehensive post-acute spectrum of care and services;
- Acute care partners in data sharing agreements;
- The utilization of CMSs—or some other—Continuity Assessment Record and Evaluation (CARE) unified patient assessment tool vs. site-specific assessment tools.

All provider services across the spectrum would also be required to use the assessment tool and be compatible with the others. Care would be coordinated by a Care Manager who is paid on per member per month basis to manage care. Requirements include 24-hour telephonic availability, monthly telephonic care conferences, in-person quarterly care conferences with the patient in the care setting, and in-person care conferences with the patient and the physician. Attached please find a more detailed paper on the concept.

Improve Care in Residential Settings

15. **Better provision of care in residential settings.** Long-term care is a residence issue as much as it is a service delivery issue. Just as care for dual eligibles is complex and inefficient, the historic separation of the streams of funding for housing and care delivery has impeded the most effective use of public moneys. Traditionally publicly financed housing and disability care providers worked separately, with little acknowledgment that they were serving the same clients, often in the same places. More recently some efforts at recognition of common clients have been instituted in public housing. A more current initiative is the provision of services, including employment initiatives, within HUD Section 811 supportive housing for younger persons with disabilities. By law, Sec. 811 projects must establish a relationship with the state Medicaid agency to utilize appropriated funds. Consideration should be given to a similar requirement for Section 202 supportive housing for the elderly. For residents receiving Medicaid LTSS, this mandate would ensure closer coordination between the care providers and the not-for-profits who are the primary sponsors of this type of housing. With both 811 and 202 rent subsidized programs, comprehensive management of service delivery within a single housing structure can create efficiencies and produce better quality, less costly care. Studies of model programs in these housing projects will be important in demonstrating their value.

    De-institutionalization of low income persons from nursing homes to less costly community settings and prevention of their entrance into nursing facilities are vital to providing greater personal independence simultaneously with lower outlays. To the extent that Sec. 811, Sec. 202, and public housing have vacancies, they are a good resource, along with the use of Money Follows the Person dollars. Use of Assisted Living Waiver slots can also be helpful where obtainable. However, many communities lack sufficient availability of rent-subsidized units that can also provide coordinated care. Killingsworth, along with other state Medicaid policy directors, proposes utilizing FFP for limited room and board supplement as a cost neutral or cost savings use of Medicaid dollars. Consideration of a waiver to permit its use, along with research of its value, would be useful. A question also arises about premature nursing home placement based on housing finances. Richard Johnson's 8–1–13 testimony indicates that those using nursing homes under Medicaid have housing wealth of $69,000 and other finances of $34,000. Those in nursing homes without Medicaid support own homes worth $155,000, and other finances totaling $289,000. It would be worthwhile to research the extent to which the Medicaid recipients go into nursing homes because of their inability to maintain their residences safely, while those at higher incomes but with the same care needs remain at home.

Creative collaborative use of public and private dollars may also assist provision of housing and care. Currently in Ohio, a not-for-profit entity is working with the state to use Medicaid savings to help finance the capital costs of converting 75 units in an affordable independent living building to assisted living. This organization also has co-located primary care practitioners at many of its sites to supply preventive care and avoid hospitalization and nursing home placement, and has placed an adult day care program within a new tax credit affordable project. In Portland a not-for-profit has purchased four rent subsidy buildings, with plans to incorporate care, to the residents, including mental health and addiction services.

Public entities working with not-for-profits make sense. In addition to sponsoring affordable housing projects, not-for-profits often offer units to rent subsidy vouchers holders within their market rate housing. The philanthropic contributions of those affiliated with the eleemosynary institutions frequently help finance supports of low income residents.

In addition to improving living and care arrangements for low income persons with disabilities in subsidized housing, localities should be planning for the likelihood that greater numbers of elderly and other persons with disabilities at all income levels will remain in their own homes and communities. One initiative, identification of Naturally Occurring Retirement Communities (NORCs), allows for more efficient provision of services within a neighborhood or apartment building. NORCs can be either publicly or personally funded. Many other initiatives require no public funds. Cities should encourage planned unit developments and master planned communities at higher densities, with shops, medical facilities and amenities within easy access of those with physical disabilities or lacking personal transportation. Zoning laws should allow free standing "mother-in-law" units to be constructed in conjunction with single family homes. Other initiatives include Urban Villages, a grass-roots aging-in-place movement of neighbors and volunteers, who pay a fee to receive coordination of supportive and other services. The nexus of housing and supportive service has largely been overlooked. While this outlook appears to be changing, much needs to be done to promote care quality within defined residential settings for all income levels.

Encourage State Innovation

16. **State Innovation Recommendation.** The Commission Report should recognize that states have an important role to play as laboratories of democracy in creating LTSS solutions and programs that move beyond the public safety net of Medicaid or public subsidies for private insurance products. States already administer much of the LTSS in this country through Medicaid. Those with advanced systems are in a position to innovate and build off of existing strengths, and those innovations can then serve as models for future federal solutions.

    To this end, the Commission should not only encourage state and local experimentation in LTSS, but should also recommend that HHS set aside grant funding for state and local agencies to develop and implement LTSS innovations, perhaps through the CMS Innovation Center, that will ultimately remove some of the financial strain from the Medicaid system. States could open up registries and infrastructure on a FFS basis to connect workers and those in need, advise on the array of community-based options through case management, the AAAs and ADRCs to expanded populations, and develop state-based funding and delivery models outside of Medicaid in order to provide an affordable and accountable means of access to services especially for the middleand lower-income populations, similar to what has been proposed and is currently being explored in Hawaii.
17. **Expand CMMI demonstration authority and funding to test models of care that fully connect home and community-based services and their associated workforce with medical care** for

people with chronic health conditions and functional limitations. An example could include incorporating the following four key components into Accountable Care Organizations: (a) comprehensive health and functional assessment; (b) creation and execution of a personalized plan of care that includes a flexible range of benefits including long-term services and supports; (c) a multidisciplinary care team tailored to the individual's needs; and (d) active involvement of family caregivers including assessing their needs and competencies.

18. **Flexibility for the states.** The diversity of the states is a challenge when trying to develop a top-down solution, but it can be an asset that can be harnessed to deliver better, more affordable patient-centered care.

    States have demonstrated their ability to develop creative solutions. Witness Gary Alexander said that the requirement in Medicaid for multiple waiver requests creates inefficiencies and poorer outcomes. He described his experience with the demonstration global waiver in Rhode Island that allows the state to rebalance Medicaid long-term care and increase access to home and community-based services, ensure access to medical homes providing coordinated care, promote accountability, and improve quality. The best recommendation he offered: "Have the federal government set broad parameters but encourage bottom-up solutions."

    Witness Patti Killingsworth recommended payment for limited room and board supplements in a community-based residential alternative setting, particularly for lower-income recipients. These kinds of innovations are best managed by states that can develop programs more quickly and that have a unique understanding of the resources available and the needs of their citizens.

    Other states, such as Pennsylvania, have had demonstrated success with an approach that integrates the medical home concept into a residential Continuing Care Retirement Community setting. This comprehensive approach allows physicians, advance practice nurses, and other professionals to coordinate each resident's care needs. Today's program silos and regulatory structures make this sought-after comprehensive system of care the exception rather than the norm.

19. **Expand Medicaid Waiver Programs.**
    a. Similar to the Rhode Island experience;
    b. Mandate that providers produce demonstrable outcomes.

20. **Financial Flexibility in Medicaid.** Testimony on the Rhode Island global compact waiver last week demonstrated the impact that providing greater flexibility to states can achieve in reducing Medicaid expenses. The Lewin Group's December 2011 study of the state's program found that the waiver resulted in at least $50 million in Medicaid savings—this in a small state—while increasing the access and quality of care provided to beneficiaries. And as the testimony noted, savings to the Medicaid program have continued in fiscal years 2012 and 2013.

    The Rhode Island success story should pave the way for further reforms that provide states additional flexibility in exchange for demonstrated reductions in spending. Whether in the form of a block grant, or *per capita* caps on beneficiary expenditures, states could use new flexibility from Washington to introduce reforms that will improve care while reducing costs—thus improving the fiscal outlook for state and federal governments alike.

    Critics of this approach express concern that any caps on expenditures will result in loss of coverage, access, or both for vulnerable beneficiaries. However, Rhode Island's waiver has resulted in three straight years of expenditure growth below CPI inflation, GDP growth, and national Medicaid spending—this even as the state's Medicaid caseload increased. These results strongly suggest that if given the proper flexibility, states can implement policies that slow the growth of spending—or reduce it outright on a *per capita* basis—not by harming the quality of care, but by *improving* it.

Improve Consumer Access and Assistance

21. **Options for Helping Americans Meet Their LTSS Needs.** Provide enhanced options counseling to help individuals better navigate LTSS in a "One-StopShop/No Wrong Door (NWD)" way to avoid unnecessary institutionalization, promoting access to home and community-based services (HCBS) and prevent Medicaid spend-down. This should be modeled after the "Enhanced Aging and Disability Resource Centers (ADRCs) Options Counseling Program" initiative released by HHS in 2012. States should be able to access enhanced administrative Medicaid match to build this necessary infrastructure.

    Nearly 10 million Americans of all ages need some form of long-term services and supports (LTSS), and about 70% of the people now turning 65 will need LTSS at some point during their life. Yet, when consumers experience a need for LTSS—or want to plan ahead for their LTSS—they are often confronted with a complex and bewildering maze of public and private programs administered by a wide variety of agencies and organizations operating under different, sometimes conflicting, sometimes duplicative, rules, regulations, and administrative procedures. Compounding this situation, people often confront the need for long-term support amidst a crisis, such as an unexpected injury, a hospital admission, or the collapse of a fragile unpaid caregiver support network. Under these circumstances, individuals and their families have little time to explore the many options that might be available, which may result in the unnecessary use of nursing facility and other expensive forms of LTSS. The fragmentation in our LTSS makes it difficult not only for our citizens to make informed decisions, but it also makes it challenging to ensure that our public expenditures on LTSS are deployed in the most cost-effective manner possible.

States develop Aging and Disability Resource Centers (ADRCs) programs— also known as One-Stop-Shop/No Wrong Door programs—to make it easier for consumers to learn about and access their LTSS options. The ADRCs program was based on best practices some states had developed to create "visible and trusted" sources of information, one-on-one counseling, and streamlined access to available LTSS options.

The importance of having an access program serve people of all income levels, not just those who qualify for Medicaid, since the vast majority of people who need LTSS are not Medicaid eligible but can be at high risk of "spending down" to Medicaid.

Improve Program Efficiency

22. **Require Medicare to audit and penalize hospitals who are abusing observer status.** Motivation: There has been a rapid increase in the use by hospitals of observer status instead of admitting patients. This change is quite likely caused by a desire by hospitals to avoid the many cost control and quality enhancing mechanisms employed by Medicare. The result for many patients, however, is the loss of eligibility to Medicare coverage of skilled nursing care, which only arises after three consecutive days of admitted hospital care.

Proposal: Medicare should embark on a program to rigorously audit and penalize hospitals who are abusing observer status, which could be indicated, for example, by a significant percentage increase in patients who stay longer than 18 hours, or receive significant surgical and other procedures, and so on, but are not admitted. The structure of incentives facing hospitals, such as third-party shared payment audits, should also be reviewed.

Reform Payment

23. **Site-Neutral Payments.** Currently, the Medicare system reimburses each type of post-acute care (PAC) provider according to different payment methodologies. Existing payment policies focus on phases of a patient's illness defined by a specific service site, rather than on the characteristics or care needs of the patient. As a result, patients with similar clinical profiles may be treated in different settings at different costs to Medicare. This payment system fails to encourage collaboration and coordination across multiple sites of care and provides few incentives that reward efficient care delivery. Such misalignment has been understood and acknowledged for some time.

    The U.S. Department of Health and Human Services, Congressional legislation (e.g., the Deficit Reduction Act), and the Medicare Payment Advisory Commission (MedPAC) have all examined such an approach. Most recently, MedPAC established criteria for selecting potential services related to the mix of sites used, patient severity, similarity of service definitions, and frequency of an associated emergency department visit (which raises the service costs). This year MedPAC began an examination of how Medicare could equalize payments for similar patients treated in long-term care hospitals (LTCHs) and acute-care hospitals. In his remarks to Congress in 2013, the MedPAC Executive Director indicated that equal payments for similar PAC services would build on MedPAC's work examining Medicare's payments for select ambulatory services.

    MedPAC has recommended and discussed many changes to PAC that would increase the value of Medicare's purchases and improve the coordination of care patients receive. These include site-neutral payments which would create more equity across providers in different sectors. MedPAC believes that such a change could be implemented in the near term and would serve as building blocks for broader payment reforms such as bundled payments and Accountable Care Organizations (ACOs).

24. **Move current programs to value care and accountability** versus fee-for-service or procedure-driven systems.
    a. Improve the quality of care through the development of standards based on patient outcomes;
    b. Provide incentives for quality-driven outcomes and coordination of care.
25. **Improve efficiency in current entitlement programs.**
    c. Rationalize payment systems and base them on objective uniform patient assessment versus site of care;
        i. Reduce barriers to access that foster duplicative and unnecessary care, such as the three-day stay requirement;
    d. Control access to Medicaid to ensure that the program is a definitive needs-based system;
        i. Tighten rules for eligibility for Medicaid and for SSI and SSDI.

Develop Uniform Assessment

26. **Develop a common uniform assessment under the guise of an independent cross-disciplinary team that's separate from CMS.** In order for a provider to deliver the best possible care across settings and maximize continuity of care, not only do the LTSS and PAC providers need to use the same assessment tools but they must also be used in hospitals. When hospitals use different assessment tools, not only is it difficult to track a patient's condition as he or she moves in and out of the hospital but communication between settings to understand the patient's needs and assess their condition is also compromised. As a result, the patient is less likely to receive appropriate care than when standard common clinical metrics are used.

    Neither the assessment tools currently in use nor the Continuity and Record Evaluation (CARE) tool are perfect; however, the use of standard clinical metrics across settings is extremely important both to patient care and to evaluation of quality across settings. Therefore, it is preferable to have a standard metric in place that is not quite perfect rather than to have multiple "near-perfect" different clinical metrics that do not allow for effective integration of care delivery across settings.

In order to develop comparable measures across different providers, information needs to be collected in identical ways (e.g., use the same assessment tool); otherwise it is not possible to develop quality measures that can accurately compare different providers. For example, if one provider uses five questions to assess ADLs on a five point scale and another uses four questions to assess ADLs on a four point scale, it is extremely difficult if not impossible to develop one quality measure to comparably assess both providers. Similarly, even if both providers used the same number of questions and same rating scale, if one provider collected the information at admission and again every four weeks, and another collected it at admission and discharge only, developing a quality measure to assess improvement over time between the two providers is impossible. Therefore, collecting data using the same tool and following the same information collection methodology is essential to continuity of care.

27. **Allocate current research funding to support innovation in long-term care.**
    a. HIT Standards;
    b. Telehealth;
    c. Expansion of Uniform Patient Assessment.

Improve Quality

28. **All fines collected from regulatory issues would be utilized to reward the top 10% of providers that have the highest discharge rate of dual-eligible patients back into the community following a post-acute stay.** Federal Civil Monetary Penalties (CMPs) and State CMPs/fines are imposed by the regulatory agencies that license skilled nursing facilities if a facility does not comply with regulatory standards. States are limited under federal law in how they may use federal CMPs. They can use federal CMPs to:
    - Maintain the operations of a facility, pending correction of deficiencies or closure;
    - Assist in receiverships and relocation of residents;
    - Reimburse residents for personal funds lost; and
    - Fund other projects that benefit facility residents.

    State CMPs/fines are not subject to these restrictions; their use is dictated by each state's laws. Under this concept, a fifth option would be created. States or the federal government would create a Quality Fund targeted to providers with the highest discharge rate to the community. Quality Fund could be aimed at people who utilize post-acute care and do not require a rehospitalization.

29. **Provide quality long-term services and supports for older people and people with disabilities in all settings.**
    i. Develop publically defined standards of care throughout all long-term care settings that are enforced through a public regulatory structure (in addition to market-based quality measures).
    j. Develop enforceable quality measures through an objective regulatory system.
    k. Ensure sufficient numbers of properly trained staff are present at all times in institutional settings.
        i. There is a high cost of poor care—improving the quality of care provided will improve health outcomes and overall savings when avoidable conditions and injuries are prevented.

C. Workforce Ideas

Family Caregivers

1. **Informal Caregiver support.** An AARP study estimated that at any one given point in time in 2009, about 42.1 million family caregivers in the United States provided care with ADLs and/or IADLs to adults with disabilities, and about 61.6 million were providing care at some time during that year. Yet these informal caregivers are themselves at risk from stress, physical strain, competing demands, and the financial effect of caregiving on their jobs and out-of-pocket expenses. Without their willingness to support family members, the dependency on public payment options would increase markedly.

   We can ill afford the loss or diminution of this voluntary help force. Rather, we should buttress it through assistance that will support informal caregivers: (1) Professional assessment of family caregivers to identify the information they need during transitions, and the skills and techniques they require at home to perform complex medical procedures and tasks such as lifting and bathing. (2) Provision of locally adapted phone aps to provide portable guides to community resources, Web-based technical instructions for nursing and medical care in the home, and caregiver support sites. (3) Reduction in caregiver isolation through institution of a trained Caregiver Corps (see Dr. Joanne Lynn's 7–17–13 testimony), which could be integrated into the Corporation for National and Community Service. For all supports, it is important to use evidence-based practices to ensure the most effective use of resources.

Please note: My recommendations for any changes to Medicaid LTSS assume expenditure neutrality within public sector spending. The degree of expansion of any LTSS would depend on the amount of savings that could be produced in another area, in this instance through savings associated with broader access to HCBS and through the work of informal caregivers preventing hospitalization and delaying entrance into a nursing home. Because the Commission will not have time to do fiscal analyses, any new or expanded services will require further study to verify costs and savings.

2. **Family Caregiving.** Family caregivers, including relatives, friends, partners and neighbors, are the backbone of long-term services and supports in this country—they provided an estimated $450 billion in unpaid contributions in 2009—more than total Medicaid spending that year. We must take the following steps to help support family caregivers caring for loved ones of all ages.

   Develop and implement a national strategy to recognize and bolster families in their caregiving roles. The strategy should identify specific actions that government, communities, providers, employers, and others can take. The strategy should address the following areas:

   - The unit of service in all health and LTSS settings should be redefined to include both individuals with disabilities and their family caregivers, with the person-and the family caregiver (as appropriate) treated as integral parts of interdisciplinary services teams.
   - The assessment and care planning process (including care transitions and coordination) must be person-and family-centered, not only identifying functional disabilities but also focusing on meeting personal goals for living as independently as possible.
   - All family caregivers should have access to relevant information, educational resources, referral services, training opportunities, and professionals supports;
   - When family caregivers agree to provide care and the care plan or discharge plan is dependent on them:
     - Their needs should be assessed along with the person receiving services;

   - They should be included in health information systems that list family caregivers, their contact information, and their involvement in implementing care plans; and
   - They should receive training (including on medical/nursing tasks), equipment, and support needed to carry out their roles.
- Respite options should be available to family caregivers, and employers should amend workplace policies to support caregiving by employees; and
- The financial security of family caregivers should be addressed so that they are not required to make enormous financial sacrifices to provide support to loved ones.

3. **Develop and implement a national strategy to recognize and bolster families in their care-giving roles.** As was the case with NAPA, the strategy should identify the specific actions that each agency of the federal government can take to promote great adoption.
   - Promote greater adoption of person-and family-centered care in all health and LTSS settings, with the person-and the family caregiver (as appropriate) at the center of care teams.
   - Assessment and service planning (including care transitions and coordination), involving care recipients and family caregivers.
   - Training (including on medical/nursing tasks) and other supports.
   - Information, education, referral.
   - Respite options.
   - Financial security.
   - Workplace policies and supports.
   - Building supportive communities including offering Social Impact Bonds that integrate services for transportation, housing, etc.

   Increase appropriations for Geriatric Education Centers to enhance the dementia care capabilities of primary and secondary health care workforce.

Professional Workforce

4. **All federally funded LTSS programs should be required to have a detailed plan for workforce recruitment, retention, and development as a requirement to continue to receive public funds.** Federal agencies should be directed to fund programs that improve working conditions and build career ladders. This includes directing CMS to fund and collect best practices on expanded home care

worker role pilots, and to evaluate and expand Value-Based Purchasing Demonstrations that reward nursing home staffing, and implement an RN and nursing home staffing mix that meets patient needs and prevents poor outcomes and avoidable hospitalizations.

5. **HHS should undertake a number of initiatives to ensure a more stable direct care workforce.**
    a. Institute systematic methods for, setting, rebasing, or updating payment rates for Medicaid home and community-based services create greater parity of wages and benefits across long-term care settings.
    b. Continue the development of national training standards for home care workers not covered by current federal requirements and have this serve as the minimum standard for training.
    c. Align government payment policies to create parity for reimbursing training costs across all direct-care occupations and provider types.
    d. Require states to collect workforce data including data on wages, benefits, hours, job vacancies and turnover rates.
6. **Creation of a national program to attract individuals to direct care jobs.** We propose that the Corporation for National and Community Service develop a program called Direct Care Corp, modeled on its SeniorCorp Companion program, to provide direct care services to individuals in need of LTSS. SeniorCorp currently runs a companion program that matches senior companions for 15 to 40 hours per week with two to four adult clients that live independently in their own homes. Under the Direct Care Corp model, individuals of all ages who enroll to become direct care workers would receive pre-service orientation, free training and certification, health insurance, and an hourly wage. As an incentive to participate in the program, if individuals agree to serve for a specified amount of time (2–4 years) in that direct care position they would be eligible for a Health Professions Opportunity Grant (HPOG) to receive fully subsidized training for the health care profession of their choice. HPOG provides education and training to TANF recipients and other low-income individuals for occupations in the health care field that pay well and are expected to either experience labor shortages or be in high demand. HPOG Funds may be used for participant supportive services, including financial aid, child care, and case management.

7. **Workforce—Recruit, train, and retain a stable, well-prepared, and high-quality workforce invested in LTSS by:**
   - Revising scope of practice standards to permit services to be provided by workers commensurate with a demonstration of competency:
     - Advanced practice registered nurses should be permitted to expand their practices commensurate with their training and competence.
     - Laws should permit the delegation of more services by direct care workers under the supervision of appropriate licensed personnel in home and community-based settings.
   - Requiring training in developing effective relationships as well as core competencies for direct-care workers to meet the full needs of the LTSS population, including diverse populations and those with dementia and behavioral health issues.
   - Ensuring that direct-care workers are integrated into interdisciplinary teams and encouraging worker participation in decisions related to resident care.
   - Promoting career development for direct workers through effective mentoring and providing career ladder opportunities in specialty areas, such as rehabilitation, dementia care, end-of-life care, and behavioral health.
   - Requiring nationwide criminal background checks prior to LTSS employment, except for certain individuals hired through self-directed programs.
8. **Ensure adequate numbers of quality LTSS caregivers are available and retained for community-based and facility care.**
   a. Pay living wages to caregivers in all settings;
   b. Establish a national Caregivers Work Force Advisory Panel to develop innovative and effective means of recruiting and maintaining a quality direct-care workforce;
   c. Establish minimum federal training standards for personal care aides based on current state efforts.

D. Follow-On

1. **Recommendation for mechanisms to move forward at the national level.** This Commission is severely limited by the timeframe

and resources allotted to it by Congress. While there is broad consensus among the Commissioners that LTSS in this country as it currently operates is not sufficient for current or future needs in this country, it is beyond the realistic scope of this body to propose a meaningful and comprehensive solution within the Commission's existing framework. Perhaps one of the most meaningful recommendations we can make is to propose a means for this work to continue in a meaningful and ongoing manner once the Commission has concluded. We recommend that Congress create a bipartisan LTSS reform task force, with appointed members from the Senate, House of Representatives, and the Secretary of Health and Human Services. The task force's charge should be similar to that of this Commission, and should use the Commission's work as a jumping-off point for its own. Ultimately the Task Force will draft a full report, make recommendations, and propose legislation to be voted on by Congress. Additionally, the Office of Disability, Aging and Long-Term Care at the Office of the Assistant Secretary for Planning and Evaluation (ASPE), should be charged with researching best practices and innovations at the state and local levels in LTSS around workforce, housing, access to services, LTSS education and public awareness, family caregiver support, and service delivery models to both inform the work of the Task force, and develop policy recommendations that can be pursued within HHS.

Additionally, the Commission should recommend that legislation be passed authorizing the White House Conference on Aging in 2015, and to have a focus on long-term services and supports. Decennial White House Conferences on Aging are now embedded in our national history. Past White House Conferences on Aging, first held in 1961 and again in 1971, 1981, 1995, and 2005 have been catalysts for aging policies and significant national programs such as Medicare, Medicaid, and the Older Americans Act. The conference has traditionally been a source of innovative solutions, and an opportunity delegates across the country, political backgrounds and professional experiences, and would be extremely valuable in the further development of policy work on long-term services and supports.

2. **Develop a new standing Commission** or similar national-level governmental body to address issues of the financing and delivery of long-term care services. This Commission should be housed within the Department of Health and Human Services and work in concert

with existing governmental bodies that relate to long-term care financing and delivery including the Governmental Accountability Office, MedPAC, MACPAC, the Advisory Council on Alzheimer's Research, Care, and Services, and others.

3. **The need for persistent and sustained attention to the design, development, and execution of a national LTSS plan requires the creation and support of a Long-Term Support and Services Commission with Executive and Legislative Branch and Private Sector Members.**

APPENDIX B. PUBLIC COMMENTS

- Karen Agron Flattery
- Darby Anderson, Addus HealthCare, Inc., Senior Vice President
- Mark Athon, Kansas Neurological Institute Parent and Guardian Group, President
- Alex Bardakh, MPP, AMDA, Senior Manager, Public Policy
- Libby Baxley, Sheridan, Arkansas
- Alexandra Bennewith, MPA, United Spinal Association, Vice President, Government Relations
- Katherine Berland, ANCOR
- Rachel Brainard, Broydrick & Associates, Research Associate
- Sarah Burger, RN, MPH, FAAN, The Coalition of Geriatric Nursing Organizations, Coalition Coordinator
- Doug Burr, Health Care Navigator, LLC, SVP of Finance Reimbursement & Gov't Relations
- Joe Caldwell, PhD, National Council on Aging, Director of Long-Term Services and Supports Policy
- Harris T. Capps, Major, USAF, Retired, Advocate for Intellectually Disabled Persons
- Roberta Carlin, MS, JD, American Association on Health and Disability, Executive Director
- Kyra Clements, Golden Age Technology
- Robb Cohen, Consultant to MHPA
- Caitlin Connolly, Eldercare Workforce Alliance
- Amy Cotton, GNP-BC, FNGNA, FAA, National Gerontological Nursing Association, President

- Bruce Cowan, Sacramento, CA
- Edward F. Coyle and Katy Beh Neas, Leadership Council of Aging Organizations and Consortium for Citizens with Disabilities
- Mary Kay Cowen, Marrero, LA
- John Cutler
- Jennifer Dexter, Easter Seals, Assistant Vice President, Government Relations
- Kim Dion, Westminster, CO
- Sherrie Dornberger, RN, CDP, GDCN, FACDONA, NADONA Executive Director
- Rep. Craig Eiland, Texas, District 23
- Leni and David Engels, Hollywood, FL
- Gail Fanjoy, KFI, Executive Director
- Cheryl Felak, RN, BSN, Because We Care, Beyond Inclusion
- Maureen Fitzgerald, The Arc Sarah Meeks, MSW, Lutheran Services in America Disability Network, Director of Public Policy and Advocacy
- Paul E. Forte, Long-Term Care Partners, LLC, Chief Executive Officer
- Loren M. Freeman, Provider of LTC Services, Guardian, Consumer
- Lex Frieden, National Advisory Board on Improving Health Care Services for Seniors and People with Disabilities, Convener
- David Gallagher
- Mary Gann, Little Rock, AR
- Laura Gargano, MPA, RN
- Dan Gaylin, NORC at the University of Chicago, Acting President
- Susan Goodman, National Down Syndrome Congress, Director, Governmental Affairs
- Fay Gordon, National Senior Citizens Law Center
- Stuart Yael Gordon, JD, Wellpoint
- David A. Gould, United Hospital Fund, Senior Vice President for Program
- Richard Grimes, Assisted Living Federation of America, President & CEO
- Carrie Hobbs Guiden, The Arc Tennessee
- David Hansell, KPMG LLP, Global Head, Human & Social Service Center for Excellence
- Mary M. Harroun, MS, LNHA, Geriatric Psychologist

- Dr. Linda Heard, Hot Springs, AR
- Jeff Hill
- Tamie Hopp, VOR, Director of Government Relations & Advocacy
- Julie M. Huso, VOR, Executive Director
- Terry Johnson, Little Rock, AR
- Paula Jorisch
- Kate Josephson, Advance CLASS
- Bob Kafka, Institute for Disability Access, Co-Director
- Joan Kelley, KNI Parent Guardian Group, Vice President
- Lois Sheaffer Kramer, CTRS; LNHA, Marklund, Director of Government Relations and Community Support
- Rob Kramer, MPA, Alzheimer's Association, Associate Director, Federal Affairs
- Dale Krause, Krause Financial Services
- Gary Langer, Langer Research Associates
- Sheryl A. Larson, ICI at University of MN, Senior Research Associate
- Sharon Levine, The Arc of New Jersey, Director of Governmental Affairs
- Bethany Lilly, The Bazelon Center for Mental Health Law, Policy Attorney
- James A. Lomastro, Ph.D., Larchmeadow Associates
- Joanne Lynn, Altarum
- Jerry and Eleanor March, Conway, Arkansas
- Andrea Maresca, National Association of Medicaid Directors, Director of Federal Policy and Strategy
- Carol Marshall, Healthcare Consultant; Fort Worth Texas
- Stephanie Mensh, Caregiver of Stroke Survivor, Paul Berger, Falls Church, VA
- Suzanne Mintz, Family Caregiver Advocacy, Founder
- Anne Montgomery, Altarum, Senior Policy Analyst
- Tracey Moorhead, Visiting Nurse Associations of America, President & CEO
- Sam Morgante, Genworth Financial, Government Relations
- John O'Leary, O'Leary Marketing Associates, President
- Chris Orestis, Life Care Funding
- Paraquad, INC., St. Louis, MO
- Rachel Patterson, MPA, Association of University Centers on Disabilities (AUCD), Policy Analyst
- Susan Payne, Parent Association for the Retarded of Texas, President

- Donald Putnam, Lexington, KY
- Romeo Raabe LUTCF, LTCP, The Long-Term Care Guy
- Max Richtman, National Committee to Preserve Social Security and Medicare
- Lyle T. Romer, Ph.D., Total Living Concept, Executive Director
- Jeff Rosen, National Council on Disability (NCD), Chairman
- E. Clarke Ross, DPA, American Association on Health and Disability, Public Policy Director
- Leo V. Sarkissian, The Arc of Massachusetts, Executive Director
- Marva Serotkin, The Boston Home, President and CEO
- Robin Shaffert, Caring Across Generations, Policy Director
- Phyllis Shelton, LTC Consultants, President
- Carole Sherman, Little Rock, AK
- Mary R. Sive, Montclair, NJ
- Congresswoman Louise Slaughter, United States House of Representatives
- Eric Sokol, Alzheimer's Foundation of America, VP, Public Policy
- Jeffrey L. Strully, Jay Nolan Community Services, CEO
- William Tapp, Elsevier, VP
- Morris J. Tenenbaum, Kings Harbor Multicare Center, Principal
- Libby Terry, Omnicare Inc., Director of Gov't Policy
- Debbie Toth, Rehabilitation Services of Northern California, Chief Executive Officer
- Barbara Trader, TASH, Executive Director
- Rebecca Underwood, Parent/guardian/advocate for Aaron Underwood
- Peter G. Wacht, CAE, National Academy of Elder Law Attorneys, Executive Director
- Laura E. Weidner, National MS Society, Director Federal Government Relations
- Kimberly Williams, LMSW, National Coalition on Mental Health and Aging, Chair
- Marybeth Williams, Consumer Voice
- Sue and Mike Yacovissi, Shreveport, LA
- Bob Yee, FSA, MAAA, Towers Watson, Senior Consultant

APPENDIX C. HEARINGS AND MEETINGS

Public Hearings

Thursday, June 27th at 2:00 p.m. EDT
Rayburn House Office Building, Room 2322
"The Current System for Providing Long-Term Services and Supports."
Witnesses:
Anne Tumlinson, Senior Vice President, Avalere Health
Kirsten Colello, Specialist in Health and Aging Policy, Congressional Research Service
G. William Hoagland, Senior Vice President, Bipartisan Policy Center
Marc Cohen, Chief Research and Development Officer, LifePlans, Inc.

Wednesday, July 17, 2013 at 1:30 p.m. EDT
Dirksen Senate Office Building Room 50
"Populations in Need of LTSS and Service Delivery Issues."
Panel 1: Diversity of LTSS Demand: Subpopulations and Their LTSS Needs
David Braddock, Executive Director, Coleman Institute for Cognitive Disabilities
H. Stephen Kaye, Assoc. Professor, University of California at San Francisco
Kevin Martone, Executive Director, Technology Assistance Collaborative
Robyn Stone, Executive Director, LeadingAge Center for Applied Research
Panel 2: Meeting LTSS Needs: Coordination of Care and Workforce Issues
Randall S. Brown, Vice President and Director Health Research, Mathematica
Josephina Carbonell, Senior Vice President, Independent Living Systems, LLC
Lynn Feinberg, Senior Strategic Policy Advisor, AARP Public Policy Institute
Joanne Lynn, Director, Altarum Center for Elder Care and Advanced Illness
Carol Regan, Government Affairs Director, Paraprofessional Healthcare Institute

Thursday, August 1, 2013 at 8:30 a.m. EDT
Dirksen Senate Office Building Room 562
"Strengthening Publicly and Privately Funded Long-Term Services and Supports."

Panel 1: Strengthening Medicaid LTSS
Diane Rowland, MACPAC
Patti Killingsworth, TennCare
Gary Alexander, formerly Rhode Island Office of Health and Human Services
Melanie Bella, CMS, Medicare-Medicaid Coordination Office

Panel 2: Strengthening Medicare for LTSS
Joseph Antos, American Enterprise Institute
Barbara Gage, Brookings Institution
Marilyn Moon, American Institute for Research

Panel 3: Strengthening Private Long-Term Care Insurance
David Grabowski, Harvard Medical School
Lane Kent, formerly Univita
Jason Brown, U.S. Treasury
Bonnie Burns, California Health Advocates

Panel 4: Interaction of Insurance, Private Resources, and Medicaid
Eric French, Federal Reserve Bank of Chicago
Jeffrey Brown, University of Illinois
Rich Johnson, Urban Institute
Ellen O'Brien, formerly MACPAC

Tuesday, August 20, 2013 at 1:00 p.m. EDT
Dirksen Senate Office Building Room 562
"Addressing LTSS Service Delivery and Workforce Issues."

Panel 1: Service Delivery and Provider Innovation and Issues 1:00 to 3:00 p.m.
Eric Berger, CEO, Partnership for Quality Home Healthcare
Lisa Alecxih, SVP and Director, Lewin Center for Aging & Disability Policy
Loren Colman, Assistant Commissioner, MN Department of Human Services, Continuing Care Administration
Laura Taylor, Director of the Caregiver Support Program, Department of Veterans Affairs

Panel 2: Workforce Innovation and Issues 3:00 to 5:00 p.m.
Tracy Lustig, Sr. Program Officer, Institute of Medicine

Suzanne Mintz, Founder, Family Caregiver Advocacy
Charissa Raynor, Executive Director, SEIU Healthcare NW., Training Partnership and Health Benefits Trust
Charlene Harrington, Professor Emeritus of Sociology and Nursing, University of California at San Francisco

Wednesday, September 18, 2013 at 2:00 p.m. to 4:00 p.m.
Dirksen Senate Office Building Room 106
Public Meeting to Release the Final Report

Executive Sessions

Thursday, June 27th at 8:30 a.m. to 12:45 p.m.
Social Security Advisory Board, 400 Virginia Avenue SW., Suite 625

Monday, July 8, 2013 at 4 p.m. to 6 p.m.
Teleconference

Wednesday, July 17, 2013 at 8:30 a.m. to 12:30 p.m.
SVC 202/203 (Capitol Visitors Center)

Thursday, August 1, 2013 at 8:30 a.m. to 5:30 p.m.
Dirksen Senate Office Building Room 562

Monday, August 19, 2013 at 8:30 a.m. to 5:00 p.m.
Dirksen Senate Office Building Room 562

Tuesday, August 20, 2013 at 8:30 a.m. to 5:00 p.m.
Dirksen Senate Office Building Room 562

Thursday, August 29, 2013 at 8:30 a.m. to 5:00 p.m.
Russell Senate Office Building Room 485

Monday, September 09, 2013 at 4:00 p.m. to 6:00 p.m.
Teleconference

Thursday, September 12, 2013 at 8:30 a.m. to 5:00 p.m.
Russell Senate Office Building Room 485

End Notes

[1] The index of ADLs was developed by Katz, see S. Katz, et al. Progress in the development of the index of ADL. The Gerontologist, 10:20-30, 1970.

[2] The index of IADLs was developed by Lawton and Brody, see M. Lawton and E. Brody. Assessment of older people: Self-maintaining and instrumental activities of daily living. Gerontologist, 9:179–186, 1969.

[3] Adapted from Reinhard S, Kassner E, Houser A, Mollica R. Raising Expectations: A State Scorecard on Long-Term Services and Supports for Older Adults, People with Physical Disabilities, and Family Caregivers. 2011; http://www.longtermscorecard.org/~/media/Microsite/Files/AARP_Re-inhard_Realizing_Exp_LTSS_Scorecard_REPORT_WEB_v3.pdf. Accessed August 26, 2013.

[4] H. Stephen Kaye. Non-Elderly People Needing Long-Term Services & Supports: Who are they? What services do they get? What services do they need? Testimony to the Commission on Long-Term Care. July 17, 2013.

[5] S. Kaye. Testimony to the Commission on Long-Term Care. July 17, 2013 (The data presented is based on Kaye's analysis of data from the 2012 National Health Interview Survey & 2010 Census and represents those who use LTSS in community settings).

[6] S. Kaye. Testimony to the Commission on Long-Term Care. July 17, 2013.

[7] Alzheimer's Association (2013). 2013 Facts and Figures. Alzheimer's Association. Retrieved from http://www.alz.org/downloads/facts_figures_2013.pdf.

[8] Alzheimer's Study Group (2009). A National Alzheimer's Strategic Plan.

[9] While age 65 is typically the dividing line between work-related disability and aging since eligibility for income security benefits and related Medicare and Medicaid is typically based on inability to work before age 65 and retirement after age 65, the division at age 65 is not a bright line—functional impairment that impedes work can be a factor for workers and potential workers at any age.

[10] D. Rowland. Testimony to the Commission on Long-Term Care. August 1, 2013.

[11] S. Kaye. Testimony to the Commission on Long-Term Care. July 17, 2013.

[12] D. Braddock. Testimony to the Commission on Long-Term Care. July 17, 2013.

[13] Congressional Budget Office. (2013). Rising Demand for Long-Term Services and Supports for Elderly People. Washington, DC: Congressional Budget Office.

[14] Ness, J., Ahmed, A., Aronow, W.S. (2004). Demographics and payment characteristics of nursing home residents in the United States: A 23 year trend. *Journals of Gerontology*, 59A (11):1213–1217. National Center for Health Statistics. (2009). National Nursing Home Survey: 2004 Overview. Washington, DC.

[15] Z. Feng, M. Fennell, D. Tyler, M. Clark, V. Mor. (2011). Growth of racial and ethnic minorities in U.S. nursing homes driven by demographics and possible disparities in options. Health Affairs, 30, 1358-1365.

[16] Murtaugh, C.M., Kemper, P., & Spillman, B.C. (1990). The risk of nursing home use in later life. *Medical Care, 28*, 952-962.

[17] Smith, D.B., Feng, Z., Fennel, M.L., Zinn, J.S., & Mor, V. (2007). Separate and unequal: Racial segregation and disparities in quality across U.S. nursing homes. *Health Affairs*.

[18] Kaye, H.S. (2013). Disability rates for working-age adults and for the elderly have stabilized, but trends for each mean different results for costs. Health Aff (Millwood), 32, 127–134; Freedman, V. A., B. C. Spillman, P. M. Andreski, J. C. Cornman, E. M. Crimmins, et al. (2013). "Trends in late-life activity limitations in the United States: an update from five national surveys." Demography 50(2): 661-671.

[19] Alzheimer's Association, "Alzheimer's disease facts and figures"(2013).

[20] An estimated 62 million family caregivers provided care at some time during the year in 2009. L. Feinberg. Populations in Need of LTSS and Service Delivery Issues. Testimony to the Commission on Long-Term Care. July 17, 2013.

[21] L. Feinberg, S. Reinhard, A. Houser, R. Choula. Valuing the Invaluable: 2011 Update: The Growing Contributions and Costs of Family Caregiving. 2011; http://assets.aarp.org/rgcenter/ppi/ltc/i51-caregiving.pdf.

[22] National Health Policy Forum. National Spending for Long-Term Services and Supports (LTSS), 2011. February 1, 2013.

[23] L. Feinberg, S. Reinhard, A. Houser, R. Choula. Valuing the Invaluable: 2011 Update: The Growing Contributions and Costs of Family Caregiving. 2011; http://assets.aarp.org/rgcenter/ppi/ltc/i51-caregiving.pdf.

[24] Pew Research Center. Social and Demographic Trends: The Decline of Marriage and the Rise of New Families. November 18, 2010.

[25] Two thirds of older adults with disabilities who receive care at home are cared for only by family members, while 26% receive both care from family members and paid help. Only 9% use paid help alone. [P. Doty. 2010]. Non-elderly adults with disabilities rely even more heavily on family caregiving—only 24% of the non-elderly population who lived alone used paid help in 2010. [S. Kaye. 2013].

[26] Feinberg op. cit.

[27] Alzheimer's Association (2013). 2013 Alzheimer's Disease Facts and Figures. Chicago, IL: Alzheimer's Association.

[28] S. Reinhard, C. Levine and S. Samis (2012). Home Alone: Family Caregivers Providing Complex Chronic Care. AARP Public Policy Institute and United Hospital Fund. http://www.aarp.org/content/dam/aarp/research/public_policy_institute/health/home-alone-family-caregivers-providing-complex-chronic-care-rev-AARP-ppi-health.pdf.

[29] D. Redfoot, L. Feinberg, and A. Houser. The Aging of the Baby Boom and the Growing Care Gap: A Look at Future Declines in the Availability of Family Caregivers. AARP Public Policy Institute. August 2013. http://www.aarp.org/content/dam/aarp/research/public_policy_institute/ltc/2013/baby-boom-and-the-growing-care-gap-insight-AARP-ppi-ltc.pdf.

[30] Gitlin, L.N., Szanton, S.L., & DuGoff, E.H. (2011). The SCAN Foundation CLASS Technical Assistance Brief No. 1: Supporting Individuals with Disability Across the Lifespan at Home: Social Services, Technologies, and the Built Environment. Retrieved from http://www.thescanfoundation.org/sites/default/files/TSF_CLASS_TA_No1_ Supporting_ Individuals_At_Home_FINAL.pdf.

[31] S. Kaye. Testimony to the Commission on Long-Term Care, July 17, 2013.

[32] *Olmstead v. L.C. 527 U.S. 581 (1999).*

[33] S. Kaye. Testimony to the Commission on Long-Term Care, July 17, 2013.

[34] Bodenheimer T. Long-Term Care for Frail Elderly People—The On Lok Model. New England Journal of Medicine. 1999; 341(17):1324–8.

[35] M. Bella. What Would Strengthen Medicaid LTSS? Testimony to the Commission on LongTerm Care. August 1, 2013; CMS MMCO Financial Alignment Initiative. Retrieved from http://www.cms.gov/Medicare-Medicaid-Coordination/Medicare-and-Medicaid-Coordination/Medicare-Medicaid-Coordination-Office/FinancialModelstoSupportStates EffortsinCareCoordination.html.

[36] L. Colman. Statement on Service Delivery and Provider Innovation and Issues. Testimony to the Commission on Long-Term Care. August 20, 2013.

[37] O'Keeffe, J., P. Saucier, B. Jackson, R. Cooper, E. McKenney, S. Crisp, et al. (2010). Understanding Medicaid Home and Community Services: A Primer. Assistant Secretary for Planning and Evaluation, U. S. Health and Human Services. http://aspe.hhs.gov/daltcp/reports/2010/primer10.pdf. Newcomer, R., T. Kang and J. Faucett (2011). "Consumer-directed personal care: comparing aged and non-aged adult recipient health-related outcomes among those with paid family versus non-relative providers." Home Health Care Serv Q 30(4): 178–197.

Caldwell, J. and T. Heller (2007). "Longitudinal outcomes of a consumer-directed program supporting adults with developmental disabilities and their families." Intellect Dev Disabil 45(3): 161–173.

[38] Wiener, J. M., W. L. Anderson and G. Khatutsky (2007). "Are consumer-directed home care beneficiaries satisfied? Evidence from Washington state." Gerontologist 47(6): 763–774.

[39] Scherzer, T., A. Wong and R. Newcomer (2007). "Financial management services in consumer-directed programs." Home Health Care Serv Q 26(1): 29–42.

[40] Institute for the Future of Aging Services (2007). The Long-term Care Workforce: Can the Crisis Be Fixed? Retrieved from http://www.leadingage.org/uploadedFiles/Content/About/Center_for_Applied_Research/Center_for_Applied_Research_Initiatives/LTC_Workforce_Commission_Report. pdf.

[41] Eldercare Workforce Alliance. Geriatrics Workforce Shortage: A Looming Crisis for Our Families. Washington, DC: Eldercare Workforce Alliance.

[42] Institute for the Future of Aging Services.

[43] PHI (2011). Facts 3: Who Are Direct Care Workers? Bronx, NY: PHI.

[44] The American Geriatrics Society. (2012). Projected Future Need for Geriatricians.

[45] ADGAP Status of Geriatrics Workforce Study, American Geriatrics Society (2008). http://www.americangeriatrics.org/files/documents/gwps/Table%201_29.pdf

[46] T Lustig. Testimony to the Commission on Long-Term Care. August 20, 2013.

[47] American Health Care Association (2011). 2011 Staffing Survey Report. Washington, DC: American Health Care Association.

[48] PHI (2012). Facts 3; America's Direct Care Workforce. Bronx, NY: PHI.

[49] National Center for Health Workforce Analysis, 2004.

[50] Institute of Medicine (2008). Retooling for an Aging America.

[51] Seavey, D. & A. Marquand (2011); American Health Care Association (2011). 2010 AHCA Survey: Nursing Facility Staffing Survey 2010. American Health Care Association; Hewitt, A. and C. Larson. (2007). The Direct Support Workforce in Community Supports to Individuals with Developmental Disabilities: Issues, Implications, and Promising Practices. Mental Retardation and Developmental Disability Research Reviews 13 (7):178–187. National Center for Assisted Living (2012). Findings from the NCAL 2011 Assisted Living Staff Vacancy, Retention, and Turnover Survey. Institute of Medicine (2008). Retooling for an Aging America.

[52] American Health Care Association (2011). Nursing Facility Staffing Survey 2010; National Center for Assisted Living (2012). Findings from the NCAL 2011 Assisted Living Staff Vacancy, Retention, and Turnover Survey.

[53] Seavey, D., & A. Marquand (2011).

[54] PHI. (2011). State Chart Book on Wages for Personal Care Aides 2000–2010. Retrieved from http://www.pascenter.org/documents/PCA_Wage_Chart_Book_2000_2010.pdf.

[55] Seavey & Marquand, 2011; Mickus, M., C.C. Luz, and A. Hogan. (2004). Voices from the Front: Recruitment and Retention of Direct Care Workers in Long-Term Care across Michigan. Michigan State University.

[56] Seavey, D. and A. Marquand, 2011

[57] Dawson, 2007. Recruitment and Retention of Paraprofessionals. PHI.

[58] Institute of Medicine (2008). Retooling for an Aging America. Institute of Medicine.

[59] IOM, 2008; A. Marquand (2013). Personal Care Aide Training Requirements. PHI. Retrieved from http://www.phinational.org/research-reports/personal-care-aide-training-requirements-sum-mary-state-findings.

[60] Seavey & Marquand, 2011.

[61] Testimony of Carol Regan. Hearing on Population in Need of LTSS and Service Delivery Issues. July 17th, 2013.

[62] Dawson, 2007. Recruitment and Retention of Paraprofessionals. Paraprofessional Health Institute.

[63] Seavey & Marquand, 2011; Castle, N.G., Engberg, E., Anderson, R.A., & Meng, A. (2007). Job satisfaction of nursing aides in nursing homes: Intent to leave and turnover. Gerontologist, 47:193– 204.

[64] For persons that need LTSS and their families, the cost of paid assistance can be substantial. According to the Genworth's 2013 Cost of Long-Term Care Survey, the median private pay daily rate in a nursing home is $207 for a shared room and $280 for a private room, though prices vary widely depending upon location and provider. According to the 2012 Eljay Survey of State Nursing Home payment rates across the United States, Medicaid programs pay an average rate of $178 per day ($7.42/hr) for 24-hour nursing services in a nursing home. For assisted living facilities, the average daily rate is approximately $117/day or less than $5.00/hour. Meanwhile, the median hourly prices of homemaker and home health services were $18 and $19 an hour, respectively—although individuals accessing home care use services on a limited number of hours per day compared to facility-based care. [From Genworth (2013). 2013 Cost of Care Survey: Home Care Providers, Adult Day Health Care Facilities, Assisted Living Facilities and Nursing Homes. Retrieved from https://www.genworth.com/dam/Americas/US/PDFs/Consumer/corporate/130568_032213_Cost%20 of%20Care_Final_nonsecure.pdf and Eljay, LLC (2012). A Report on Shortfalls in Medicaid Funding for Nursing Center Care. Retrieved from http://www.ahcancal.org/research_data/funding/Documents/2012%20Report%20on%20Shortfalls%20in%20Medicaid%20Funding%20for%20Nursing%20Home%20Care.pdf].

[65] D. Braddock. 2013.

[66] S. Kaye. 2013.

[67] Kemper, P., Komisar, H.L., & Alecxih, L. (2005/2006). Long-term care over an uncertain future: What can current retirees expect? *Inquiry, 42*, 335–350.]

[68] Kemper, P., Komisar, H.L., & Alecxih, L. (2005/2006). Long-term care over an uncertain future: What can current retirees expect? *Inquiry, 42*, 335–350. Costs are in 2005 dollars.

[69,70] Feder J, Komisar H. The Importance of Federal Financing to the Nation's Long-Term Care Safety Net. (2012) p. 3.

[71] James M. Poterba, Steven F. Venti, David A. Wise, "Were They Prepared for Retirement? Financial Status at Advanced Ages in the HRS and AHEAD Cohorts, NBER Working Paper No. 17824 (February 2012).

[72] Associated Press-NORC Center for Public Affairs Research (April 2013). Long-Term Care Poll: Perceptions, and Attitudes among Americans 40 or Older. http://www.thescanfoundation.org/associated-press-norc-center-public-affairs-research-long-term-care-poll-perceptions-and-attitudes; Langer Research Associates (August 2013). Pathways to Progress in Planning for Long-Term Care. http://www.thescanfoundation.org/sites/thescanfoundation.org/files/langer-ltcpoll-analysis-8-15-13.pdf.

[73] Brown, J.R. and A. Finkelstein (2004). Supply or Demand: Why is the Market for Long-Term Care Insurance So Small? National Bureau of Economic Research. Retrieved from http://www.nber. org/papers/w10782.

[74] M. Cohen. Testimony to the Commission on Long-Term Care. June 27, 2013.

[75] CalPers LTCI (a California State Employee group insurance) raised premiums 22 percent in 2009 and recently announced another 85 percent increase in premiums. R. G. Frank, M. Cohen & N. Mahoney (2013). Making Progress: Expanding Risk Protection for Long-Term Services and Supports through Private Long-Term Care Insurance. SCAN Foundation. http://www.thescanfoundation.org/sites/thescanfoundation.org/files/tsf_ltc-financing_private-options_frank_3-20-13.pdf

[76] In the Commission's August 20 public hearing, J. Brown testified that given crowd-out, all but the highest 10 to 35 percent of the wealth distribution would be rational not to buy private LTCI. [J. Brown. Testimony to the Commission on Long-Term Care. August 20, 2013]. Brown also noted that a separate study comparing showed that states with more generous Medicaid eligibility had lower rates of private LTCI coverage. (Brown, J.R., Coe, N.E., & Finkelstein, A. (2007). Medicaid Crowd-Out of Private Long-Term Care Insurance

Demand: Evidence from the Health and Retirement Survey. In J.M. Poterba (ed.), *Tax Policy and the Economy* (1–31). Cambridge, MA: MIT Press.) D. Grabowski testified that crowd-out is rational and likely at low asset levels (bottom tercile), but not at middle and upper asset levels—citing buyer/non-buyer data that shows a big uptake in private insurance between $50,000 and $100,000 in assets. Grabowski also noted that even with Brown and Finkelstein estimates of crowd-out, 40 percent of the population would still be candidates for private LTCI. (D. Grabowski. Testimony to the Commission on Long-Term Care. August 20, 2013).

[77] Assistant Secretary for Planning and Evaluation (2012). Long-Term Care Insurance: ASPE Research Brief. Assistant Secretary for Planning and Evaluation, U.S. Department of Health and Human Services. Retrieved from http://aspe.hhs.gov/daltcp/reports/2012/ltcinsRB.shtml#note26.

[78] CBO, 2013. Exhibit 20.

[79] America's Health Insurance Plans (2012). Who Buys Long-Term Care Insurance in 2010–2011? America's Health Insurance Plans. Retrieved from http://www.ahip.org/Issues/Long-Term-Care-Insurance.aspx.

[80] M. Warshawsky. The Life Care Annuity: A proposal for an insurance product innovation to simultaneously improve financing and benefit provision for long-term care and to insure the risk of outliving assets in retirement. Working Paper No. 2. Long-Term Care Financing Project, Health Policy Institute, Georgetown University. June 2007.

Murtaugh, C.M., Spillman, B.C., & Warshawsky, M. (2001). In sickness and in health: An annuity approach to financing long-term care and retirement income. *The Journal of Risk and Insurance, 68* (2), 225–254.

Brown, J., & Warshawsky, M. (2013). The life care annuity: A new empirical examination of an insurance innovation that addresses problems in the markets for life annuities and long-term care insurance. *Journal of Risk and Insurance, 80* (3), 677–704.

[81] Dual Eligibles: Medicaid's Role for Low-Income Medicare Beneficiaries. Kaiser Commission on Medicaid and the Uninsured. Fact Sheet May 2011.

[82] Kaiser Family Foundation. Medicaid's Long-Term Care Users: Spending Patterns Across Institutional and Community-based Settings. October 2011. http://kaiserfamilyfoundation.files.wordpress.com/2013/01/7576-02.pdf. page 3.

[83] Medicaid eligibility is complicated and varies substantially from state to state. For states that base eligibility on the federal SSI coverage requirements, in 2013 recipients must have monthly income below $710 for an individual ($1,066 for a couple), about 75 percent of the federal poverty level (FPL). States may extend Medicaid coverage to individuals in a nursing home or other institution with incomes up to 300 percent of FPL. Under SSI program rules, Medicaid recipients may also have countable assets of no more than $2,000 for an individual (no more than $3,000 for a couple). Medicaid allows the recipient to exclude the value of the primary residence (up to $536,000 in 2013, although states can allow up to $802,000 in 2013) as well as a car and personal and household items and burial funds and term life insurance, and, in many states, qualified retirement assets in distribution status, from countable assets. States may use more restrictive income and asset rules, and there are some states with less restrictive rules. (K. Colello, Congressional Research Service, Testimony before the Commission on Long-Term Care, June 27, 2013). The Medicaid estate recovery program allows states to recoup private assets when a beneficiary dies in order to recover Medicaid expenditures on that person's behalf. The amount of recovery through this program has been relatively small, but varies among states. (Julie Stone, CRS Report for Congress, Medicaid Coverage for Long-Term Care: Eligibility, Assets Transfers, and Estate Recovery, January 2008).

[84] U.S. Government Accountability Office, *Medicaid Transfers of Assets by Elderly Individuals to Obtain Long-Term Care Coverage*. GAO–05–968 (Washington, DC: U.S. Government Accountability Office, September 2005).

[85] K. Colello, Congressional Research Service, Testimony before the Commission on LongTerm Care, June 27, 2013. The CRS testimony provided an extensive discussion of asset transfer and estate recovery rules and state variation in rules and compliance. E. O'Brien. (2013). Interaction of Insurance, Private Resources, and Medicaid: Assessing the Evidence. Testimony before Commission on Long Term Care. August 1. http://www.ltccommission.senate.gov/Ellen%20O%27Brien%20PP. pdf; Stone, J. (2008). Medicaid Coverage for Long-Term Care: Eligibility, Asset Transfers, and Estate Recovery. RL33593. January 31. http://www.aging.senate.gov/crs/medicaid18.pdf; Stone, J. (2011). Medicaid Eligibility for Persons Age 65+ and Individuals with Disabilities: 2009 State Profiles. Congressional Research Service. Report,R41899. June 28. http://www. pascenter.org/documents/medicaid_eligibility.pdf.

[86] National Health Policy Forum. National Spending for Long-Term Services and Supports (LTSS), 2011. February, 2013. Available data underestimates the amount of out-of-pocket (OOP) spending for LTSS because existing surveys do not capture all OOP spending on LTSS (for example, OOP spending for assisted living is not reported, although it may be substantial).

[87] In addition, 4 percent pays for mental health services and intermediate care facilities for persons with intellectual disabilities. Kaiser Family Foundation. Medicaid and its Role in State/Federal Budgets & Health Reform. April 2013. http://kaiserfamilyfoundation.files.wordpress. com/2013/04/8162-03.pdf. Figure 18.

[88] S. Eiken, et al. Medicaid Expenditures for Long-Term Services and Supports: 2011 Update. Thomson Reuters. October 2011.

[89] Kaiser Family Foundation. How Much Will Medicaid Cost in the Future and Why: A Look at Federal Projections. August 2013. Figure 8.

[90] Kaiser Family Foundation. Medicaid and its Role in State/Federal Budgets & Health Reform. April 2013. http://kaiserfamilyfoundation.files.wordpress.com/2013/04/8162-03. pdf. Figure 32.

[91] Congressional Budget Office. The 2012 Long-Term Budget Outlook. June 2012. P. 58. The projections as a share of GNP are for the combination of federal spending for Medicaid, CHIP, and tax credits for health insurance purchase under the ACA.

[92] Congressional Budget Office. Rising Demand for Long-Term Services and Supports for Elderly People. June 2013. Exhibit 16.

[93] Saucier, P., B. Burwell, A. Halperin and H. Butera (2013). Consumer Choices and Continuity of Care in Managed Long-Term Services and Supports: Emerging Practices and Lessons. AARP. 2013–07. July.

Cheek, M., M. Roherty, L. Finnan, E. G. Cho, J. Walls, K. Gifford, et al. (2012). On the Verge: The Transformation of Long-Term Services and Supports. AARP Public Policy Institute. http://www.aarp.org/content/dam/aarp/research/public_policy_institute/ltc/2012/On-the-Verge-The-Transformationof-Long-Term-Services-and-Supports-Report-AARP-ppi-ltc.pdf.

[94] Saucier, P., J. Kasten, B. Burwell and L. Gold (2012). The Growth of Managed Long-Term Services and Supports (MLTSS) Programs: A 2012 Update. Prepared for the Centers for Medicare & Medicaid Services (CMS), Disabled and Elderly Health Programs Group under Contract #: HHSM500-2005-00025I, Task Order No. 0002. July. <http://www.medicaid.gov/Medicaid-CHIP-Program-Information/By-Topics/Delivery-Systems/Downloads/MLTSSP_White_paper_combined.pdf>.

[95] Of 3.5 million families with a member with a severe and chronic disability expected to last a lifetime, only 13% are supported by the states' public agency services (Braddock, Presentation to AIDD, February 2013)

[96] In a national survey conducted by the Arc of the United States, 82% of families reported that their overall economic security is challenged. 73% reported not having adequate savings for retirement, which puts aging parents in particularly vulnerable situations. (*Still in the Shadows with Their Futures Uncertain*, Arc of the US, June 2011). According to Braddock

(2013, above) there are 853,000 persons with developmental disabilities/intellectual disabilities (DD/ID) living at home with caregivers over the age of 65 years.

[97] Income earned grows tax free; withdrawals for qualified disability expenses are tax free; there are rollover provisions to traditional 529 accounts or other family members, ABLE or 529 Accounts; and the same reporting requirements apply as to a traditional 529.

[98] MBI programs allow people to work and save and maintain access to Medicaid while paying co-pays based on income. Most states have MBI programs, but income and resource limits vary significantly. 1619(b) programs allow people to maintain Medicaid access while working but do not change resource limits. Every state participates in 1619(b), but income limits vary significantly.

In: Long-Term Care
Editor: Kevin Pickens
ISBN: 978-1-63117-108-6

Chapter 2

FACTORS AFFECTING THE DEMAND FOR LONG-TERM CARE INSURANCE: ISSUES FOR CONGRESS*

Janemarie Mulvey

SUMMARY

As the 80 million baby boomers approach retirement, many are concerned they will not have sufficient savings to sustain their standard of living in retirement. Few, however, may be focused on another risk to their retirement security—the potential cost of financing often expensive longterm care services and supports (LTSS). LTSS include help with either functional or cognitive impairment and generally include assistance with activities such as bathing, eating, and dressing. For the majority of older Americans, the cost of obtaining paid help for these services may far exceed their financial resources in the future.

Private long-term care insurance (LTCI) is available to provide some financial protection for persons against the risk of the potentially high cost of LTSS. In 2010, about 6% of LTSS spending was paid by LTCI. This low rate of financing reflects relatively low demand for LTCI over the past few decades. Moreover, most policy owners have not yet reached the age where they may need services.

* This is an edited, reformatted and augmented version of a Congressional Research Service publication, CRS Report for Congress R40601, prepared for Members and Committees of Congress, from www.crs.gov, dated January 16, 2013.

In 2010, between 7 million to 9 million Americans owned a private LTCI policy, with about 11% of the population aged 55 and older covered by a policy. A number of factors have adversely affected the demand for LTCI. The cost and complexity of LTCI policies have been cited as major deterrents to purchasing LTCI. In addition, increased concerns have arisen about the adequacy of consumer protections for LTCI as a result of inconsistencies in LTCI laws and regulations across the states. More recently, adverse publicity about premium increases and heightened concerns about the future solvency of LTCI insurers in the current economic environment have further dampened demand, prompting state regulators to re-evaluate current regulations and laws governing LTCI.

The private LTCI market has undergone significant changes in the past three decades. The employer-sponsored market has grown as a share of total LTCI sales and the overall market has become more concentrated in terms of the number of companies selling the product. A number of newer product lines have been introduced that combine LTCI with other products, such as retirement annuities and life-insurance products.

To address these issues, the 113th Congress may consider a number of legislative options to increase participation in the voluntary LTCI market. These may include proposals to

- increase tax incentives to lower the after-tax cost of policies,
- improve consumer protections to boost consumer confidence in the product, and
- expand consumer education.

This report discusses the role of LTCI in financing LTSS and current trends in the LTCI industry; factors affecting the demand for LTCI, including cost and complexity of the product and adequacy of consumer protections; and legislative options available to address these issues.

INTRODUCTION

As the 80 million baby boomers approach retirement, many are concerned they will not have sufficient savings to sustain their standard of living throughout retirement. Few, however, have focused on another risk to their retirement security—the potential cost of financing often expensive long-term care services.

The cost of long-term services and supports (LTSS) for the majority of older Americans may far exceed their financial resources in the future. Private longterm care insurance (LTCI) is available to provide some financial protection for persons against the risk of the potentially high cost of LTSS. To date, however, only about 1 in 10 individuals aged 55 and older own a LTCI policy.

This report discusses

- the role of LTCI in financing LTSS and current trends in the LTCI industry;
- factors affecting the demand for LTCI, including cost and complexity of the product and adequacy of consumer protections; and
- legislative options available to improve affordability, strengthen consumer protections, and expand consumer education.

PRIVATE LONG-TERM CARE INSURANCE

Services provided by a LTCI policy may include a broad range of services and supports to help people with a limited capacity for self-care due to a physical, cognitive (such as Alzheimer's disease), or mental disability or condition. Health care and LTSS are different. Health care services typically treat specific acute and chronic medical conditions in a medical setting by a medical professional. LTSS, on the other hand, include a wide range of health and health-related support services provided on an informal or formal basis to people who have functional disabilities or cognitive impairments over an extended period of time with the goal of maximizing their independence.[1] Unlike medical treatments, LTSS primarily assist individuals in their day-to-day activities.

These "activities of daily living" (ADLs) include bathing, dressing, eating, toileting, and transferring (from a bed to a chair or vice-versa). Generally, LTCI policyholders are eligible to begin to receive benefits if they have at least two of the ADL limitations.

LTCI policies may be sold to an individual directly or to a group as part of an employer-sponsored policy. The premiums charged for LTCI vary by age of purchase, with higher premiums charged to those purchasing at older ages. This age differential reflects the higher risk of needing LTSS at advanced ages. One study has estimated that over two-thirds of individuals who turn 65 years old will require LTSS at some point before they die.[2]

Current Financing of Long-Term Services and Supports

Although private LTCI is available to finance LTSS costs, only about 6% of LTSS spending was paid by LTCI in 2010. Nearly half of LTSS spending (nearly 43%) was financed by the Medicaid program, which is funded jointly by the federal government and states.[3] Medicaid is intended to provide a safety net and is not available to everyone. To be eligible, individuals must meet certain functional criteria as well as state-specified income and asset thresholds.[4] Medicare (which currently provides health care to older Americans and certain disabled individuals) financed about 22% of LTSS, but these funds were predominantly for post-acute care for short-stays in a skilled nursing home following hospitalization or for skilled home health care.

Individuals who seek paid LTSS but do not qualify for public funding or do not have private LTCI must pay for these services directly out-of-pocket. In 2010, about 16% of LTSS spending was paid out-of-pocket.[5] The magnitude of out-of-pocket costs will depend on the setting, intensity (including the skill level of the provider), and the duration of LTSS. For example, the setting of care can include care provided in one's own home, in a community-residential care setting such as an assisted living facility, or in an institutional setting such as a nursing home. For those receiving care at home, in 2012, the average cost of personal unskilled care (such as bathing, dressing, and transferring) was $19 an hour.[6] Studies have found that individuals use on average about 18.4 hours a week of informal care, which would result in an annual cost of about $18,179 a year in 2012. The annual cost of care will also vary by intensity and duration of care, with individuals receiving care in an institutional setting paying more than those staying at home. For example, assisted living facilities that provide hands-on personal care for those who are not able to live by themselves (but do not yet require constant care provided by a nursing home) cost on average $39,600 annually in 2012. Nursing home care, on the other hand, generally costs more in that it provides LTSS assistance 24 hours a day. In 2012, the annual cost of a nursing home stay was $73,000 for a semi-private room and $81,030 for a private room.[7] These estimates are national figures and can vary widely by geographic region.

Long-Term Care Insurance Industry Trends

The private LTCI market has undergone significant changes in the past three decades. The employer-sponsored market has grown as a share of total

LTCI sales and the overall market has become more concentrated in terms of the number of companies selling the product. Further, a number of newer product lines have been introduced that combine LTCI with other retirement and life-insurance products. The following discussion provides greater details on these trends.

There are currently between 7 million to 9 million Americans with an active LTCI policy (often called "in-force").[8] The growth in the number of LTCI policies in both the individual and group markets increased at double-digit rates from 1995 to 2002 before slowing in more recent years (see Figure 1). The composition of the market has also changed as employer-sponsored LTCI has grown as a share of the total LTCI market. In 2011, employer-sponsored LTCI represented about one-third of all active policies, compared with less than 3% in the mid-1990s. Employer-sponsored LTCI is distinct from employer-sponsored health insurance in that employers typically do not contribute to LTCI premiums. Rather employer-sponsored LTCI provides the advantage of a larger risk pool and generally lower premiums than if LTCI is purchased in the individual market. Among employers offering LTCI, the federal government is the largest employer offering group LTCI.

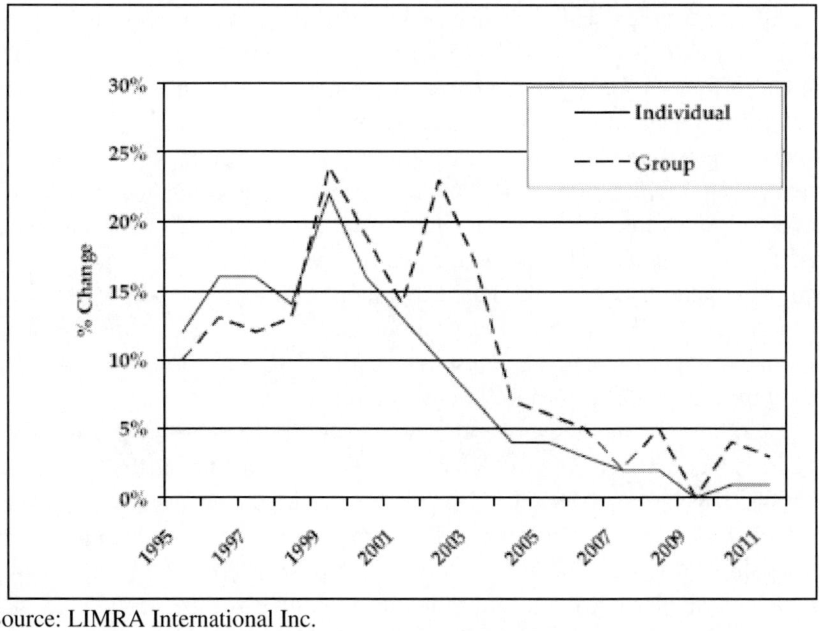

Source: LIMRA International Inc.

Figure 1. Percentage Change in Growth of Active LTCI Policies, 1995-2011.

Over the past decade, the number of companies selling LTCI has declined significantly. Between 1987 and 2002, more than 100 companies were selling LTCI. A downturn in sales beginning in 2003 prompted many insurers to exit the market or merge with other firms.[9] As a result, the LTCI market has become much more concentrated, with the top 10 LTCI companies producing 88% of new sales in 2010. [10] This number has fallen further in recent years. Since 2010, a number of well-known companies have exited the LTCI market. MetLife has announced that it has discontinued new sales of LTCI effective December 30, 2010. MetLife assured existing policyholders that their coverage will continue without any interruptions or changes. In February of 2011, Unum Group announced it will no longer sell group policies. In March of 2011, Prudential announced it will no onger sell LTCI policies to individuals and will instead focus on the group market. The consolidation of the LTCI industry reflects several factors, including high administrative expenses for policies relative to premiums, lower than expected terminations (i.e., lapse rates) that increased the number of people likely to submit claims, low interest rates that reduced the expected return on investments, and new government regulations limiting direct marketing by telephone.[11]

Hybrid Long-Term Care Insurance Products

A number of legislative changes have enabled insurers to begin to develop hybrid products that combine LTCI with either an annuity or a life insurance product. The Pension Protection Act of 2006 (P.L. 109-280) simplified tax rules regarding combination products (effective in 2010) and added a tax provision specifying that proceeds from an annuity can be used tax-free to purchase an LTCI policy. LTCI policies can also be combined with a life insurance policy through an accelerated death benefit rider. Circumstances that trigger these accelerated benefits include diagnosis of a terminal illness or a medical condition that would drastically shorten the policyholder's life span, the need for LTSS, or permanent confinement to a nursing home. Because these newer hybrid policies are just entering the market, it is too early to tell their impact on demand for LTCI in the future.

In addition to the above-mentioned hybrid LTCI policies, there is also a LTCI product that is linked to Medicaid eligibility. The Deficit Reduction Act of 2005 (DRA; P.L. 109-171)[12] established the Medicaid Partnership Long-Term Care Insurance Partnership Program (hereinafter referred to as the Partnership Program). Individuals who purchase certain LTCI policies may qualify for Medicaid without the same means-testing requirements that other applicants must meet. Generally, Partnership Program purchasers would seek Medicaid for extended coverage of LTSS after their LTCI benefits have been exhausted. For these individuals, Medicaid means-testing requirements are relaxed at (1) the time of application to Medicaid, and (2) the time of the beneficiary's death when Medicaid estate recovery is generally applied.[13,14]

The original Partnership Program was established in four states: California, Connecticut, Indiana, and New York in the early 1990s.[15] The Omnibus Budget Reconciliation Act of 1993 (OBRA 93, P.L. 103-66) prohibited other states from implementing the program. However, the Deficit Reduction Act of 2005 (DRA, P.L. 109-171) lifted this prohibition and allowed any state with a Secretary-approved Medicaid state plan amendment to operate a Partnership program.[16] As of July 2011, 40 states, including the 4 original partnership states, elected to adopt a LTCI Partnership program.17 Ten states have yet to adopt a LTCI Partnership Program.18 There are about 641,000 Partnership Program policies in force, accounting for 9% of all LTCI policies in force.[19]

FACTORS AFFECTING THE DEMAND FOR PRIVATE LONG-TERM CARE INSURANCE

After 15 years of strong growth, demand for private LTCI has slowed considerably since 2004.[20] In 2008, the latest year in which demographic data are available, about 11% of the population aged 55 and older and 12% of the population aged 65 and older owned a LTCI policy.[21] Low demand for this product has occurred despite enhanced tax incentives (mainly at the state level), increased emphasis on consumer protections, and the enactment of a private LTCI program for federal employees.

The factors affecting the demand for LTCI can be viewed by comparing two key cohorts: those under the age of 65 and those aged 65 and older. For those under the age of 65, annual LTCI premiums are generally lower.[22] However, this cohort also faces competing demands of the cost of raising families and saving for retirement. Many do not fully understand their future risks or coverage options for LTSS. According to a survey by America's Health Insurance Plans, 28% of non-buyers believe Medicare will cover their LTSS needs, and another 22% do not know who would pay.[23] Although Medicare does cover up to 100 days of care in a skilled nursing facility,[24] and limited home health care,[25] it does not cover longer stays in a nursing home or personal home care. By the time individuals reach the age of 65 or so, if they have not sufficiently planned for their LTSS needs, the cost and complexity of the LTCI policies become a major barrier to purchase. In addition, increased concerns have arisen about the adequacy of consumer protections for LTCI as a result of inconsistencies in LTCI laws and regulations across the states. More recently, adverse publicity about potential problems with premium stability, claims denials by LTCI companies, and heightened concerns about the future solvency of LTCI companies in the current economic environment have further dampened demand. The following section discusses these issues in greater detail.

Cost and Complexity of Long-Term Care Insurance

The cost of LTCI has been cited as a major deterrent to purchasing the product. Among potential buyers of LTCI who choose not to purchase a policy, 87% cite cost as a "very important" or "important" reason for their decision.[26] Over the past decade, LTCI premiums have increased significantly above the overall rate of inflation. As shown in *Table 1*, between 1995 and 2010, average age-adjusted premiums have increased 71% (above the overall rate of inflation) for individuals aged 55 to 64 and by 64% for those aged 65 to 69, growing at an annual average rate of 3.7% and 2.8% (respectively) over and above the general rate of inflation. Higher average premiums reflect increased demand for more comprehensive benefit packages (including inflation protection) and higher daily benefit amounts. In addition, low rates of return on investments and under estimates of lapse (termination) rates have prompted insurers to raise premiums for both current and new policyholders.

Although more comprehensive policies have raised annual premiums, they have also increased the complexity of the purchase decision. According to the America's Health Insurance Plans (AHIP) survey, 49% of those who did not buy an LTCI policy when given the opportunity stated that the policy options were "too confusing." Potential buyers must evaluate the many different possible combinations of product features available.

Potential policyholders must decide

- the type of coverage,
- the dollar amount of coverage and annual inflation adjustments,
- the length or duration of coverage, and
- the waiting period (which is often referred to as the elimination period).

Table 1. Average Annual Age-Specific LTCI Premiums, By Purchase Year (in 2010 Inflation-Adjusted Dollars)

					% Change 1995 to 2010	
					Annual Average	Cumulative Rate
Age	1995	2000	2005	2010	Rate	
55 to 64	$1,315	$1,536	$2,096	$2,255	3.7%	71%
65 to 69	$1,684	$1,883	$2,236	$2,759	3.3%	64%
70 to 74	$2,186	$2,316	$2,614	$3,294	2.8%	51%

Source: CRS estimates using CPI-U to adjust nominal premiums reported in America's Health Insurance Plans, "Who Buys Long-Term Care Insurance in 2010-2011? A Twenty Year Study of Buyers and Non-Buyers in the Individual Market," March 2012.

Type of Coverage

Individuals must choose the type of services to be covered by a LTCI policy. Services covered under a LTCI policy may include care in a variety of settings, such as a nursing home or assisted living facility, or the individual's own home through home health services. Policies may cover respite care for caregivers, homemaker and chore services and medical equipment. Policies purchased in 2010 tend to be more comprehensive in terms of services covered and are most likely to cover both nursing home and home care services. According to AHIP, 95% of policies purchased in 2010 covered both nursing home and home care as compared with 61% of policies purchased in 1995 (see *Table 2*).[27]

Dollar Amount of Coverage and Annual Inflation Adjustments

Another factor affecting the cost and complexity of a policy is how much coverage should be purchased in terms of a daily benefit amount and whether to purchase inflation protection. The dollar amount of the daily benefit is often initially chosen based on the current cost of services. But the decision about how much this daily benefit should be adjusted over time to reflect inflation is a more complicated one.

Inflation adjustments (often called inflation protection) are important because a LTCI policy is often purchased 20 to 30 years before services are needed. Thus, a policy purchased today that pays a $150 a day benefit may not be sufficient given growth in the cost of future LTSS. To ensure that policies cover an adequate amount of services, most companies now offer inflation protection and most public awareness campaigns have urged individuals to purchase inflation protection. As a result of these efforts, policies purchased in 2010 are more likely to include inflation protection (see *Table 2*) as compared with those purchased in 1995.

Table 2. Characteristics of LTCI Policies Purchased Since 1995

Policy Characteristics	1995	2000	2005	2010
Policy Type (% With)				
—Nursing Home Care Only	33%	14%	3%	1%
—Nursing Home & Home Care	61%	77%	90%	95%
—Home Care Only	6%	9%	7%	4%
Daily Benefit Amounts (Nominal $)				
—Nursing Home Care	$85	$109	$142	$153
—Home Care	$78	$106	$135	$152
% With Inflation Protection	33%	41%	76%	74%
—Simple	14%	17%	23%	12%
—Compound	15%	22%	49%	49%
—Indexed to CPI	4%	2%	4%	13%
Elimination Period for Nursing Home Benefit	46 days	47 days	81 days	90 days

Source: America's Health Insurance Plans, "Who Buys Long-Term Care Insurance in 2010-2011? A Twenty Year Study of Buyers and Non-Buyers in the Individual Market," March 2012.

In terms of the type of inflation protection, companies offer both simple and compound inflation adjustments. Although both methods increase the daily benefit by a fixed percentage, they vary on which year the percentage is applied. Simple inflation adjustments increase annually based on a fixed percentage of the daily benefit amount calculated from the *first year the policy is purchased*, so annual adjustments are a fixed dollar amount. Whereas compound inflation adjustments increase the daily benefit amount annually based on a fixed percentage calculated from each *previous year's* daily benefit amount (see *Figure 2*), so the annual adjustments of the daily benefit amount increase over time.

Once the policyholder chooses the type of inflation protection, he or she then must decide how much inflation-protection to purchase annually. In making this decision, one approach would be to rely on historical data. For example, since 2000, the price of nursing home care increased at an annual average rate of 4.3%. However, it is unknown whether these trends will continue in the future. Potential policyholders must decide whether they should choose inflation protection based on historical trends or choose a higher or lower rate based on expectations about the future. This decision affects both the complexity and the cost of the policy.

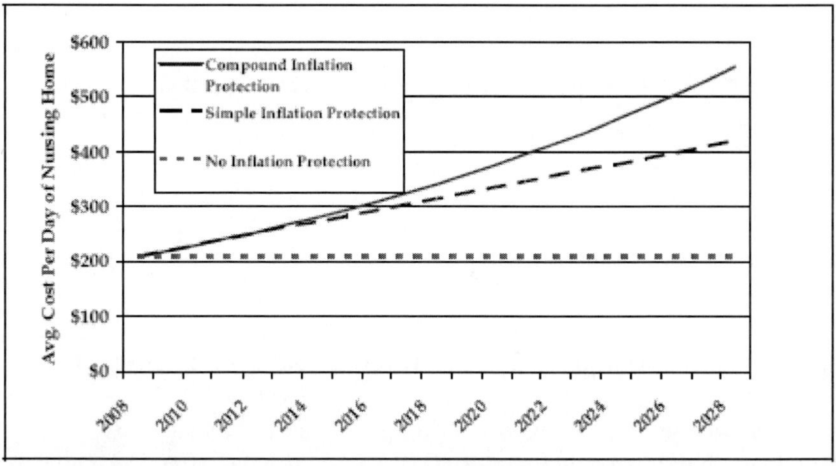

Source: CRS Estimates. Daily benefit amounts in 2008 derived from Genworth Financial 2008 Cost of Care Survey, April 2008.

Notes: Inflation adjustments assume 5% annual rate of growth.

Figure 2. Illustration of Compound vs. Simple Inflation Adjustments.

Duration of the Benefit

The length of coverage (in years) of a LTCI policy is called the *duration of the benefit*. Deciding how much coverage to purchase further complicates the decision process. LTCI policies can cover two to five years of services and some policies can provide lifetime benefits. Although potential policyholders want to purchase a policy that may sufficiently cover future risks, most do not know what that risk may be because it varies widely across the older population. For example, researchers have estimated that, of those who turned 65 years old in 2005, approximately one-third will not require any LTSS over their remaining lifetime. At the same time, one in five will require LTSS for more than five years.[28] The longer the duration of coverage, the higher the premiums.

Elimination Period

LTCI policies often have a waiting or elimination period that is the length of time between the onset of qualifying impairments and commencement of payment for LTSS. The elimination period is selected by the policyholder when he or she purchases the policy. This elimination period is conceptually similar to a deductible in a health care plan—the longer the elimination period the lower the cost of the policy, all other things equal. Policies purchased in 2010 tend to have a longer waiting ("elimination") period, as compared with 15 years earlier (see *Table 2*). Unlike other policy design features, a longer elimination period (holding other design features constant) can reduce premiums.

Adequacy of Consumer Protections For Long-Term Care Insurance Policyholders

In addition to the cost and complexity of products, there has been a growing concern that many LTCI policies do not have sufficient consumer protections. These consumer protections are important given that a LTCI policy is often purchased 20 years or longer before the actual benefit is used. This long-time horizon introduces a great deal of uncertainty regarding the nature of future benefits, long-run affordability of premiums for purchasers, and the financial stability of insurers. Many of the laws and regulations that have been established by federal and state governments attempt to address these issues. However, each state has its own set of laws and regulations and there is wide variation across states.

State Oversight

State governments have primary jurisdiction for regulating the LTCI market. To do this, states have established laws and regulations for LTCI carriers and the products they sell and play an active role in verifying carriers' and products' compliance with these requirements. To help guide states in their LTCI oversight efforts, the National Association of Insurance Commissioners (NAIC) has developed a number of "Model Laws" and "Model Regulations" (hereinafter referred to as Model provisions), which provide recommended guidelines for state lawmakers and regulators to adopt. These Model provisions are updated periodically by the state insurance commissioners. Because each state ultimately establishes its own LTCI laws and regulations, state oversight requirements are not consistent across states, leaving gaps in consumer protections. According to the NAIC, all states, with the exception of Alaska, have adopted some components of the NAIC Model provisions, but there is wide variability in which provisions were adopted.[29]

Federal Oversight

Since 1996, the federal government has attempted to standardize these regulations at a national level for certain LTCI products. Federal law has included provisions for federal tax benefits and minimum consumer protection standards for purchasers of "tax-qualified" LTCI policies as authorized by the Health Insurance Portability and Accountability Act of 1996 (HIPAA, P.L. 104- 191).[30] HIPAA tax-qualified products must conform to most of the provisions in the 1993 NAIC Model Law and Regulations. These products are also required to offer (but not mandate) inflation protection.

The Medicaid Partnership Program established under DRA (see discussion earlier about hybrid LTCI products) includes minimum consumer protection requirements for the LTCI plans sold under the Partnership Program as specified in the 2000 NAIC Model Provisions (see *Table 3*). In contrast to the HIPAA voluntary 5% compound inflation-protection requirement, the DRA provisions include a mandatory inflation-protection provision for certain age groups for the Partnership Program. DRA, however, does not specify the amount of inflation-protection that is required and instead leaves this decision up to the individual states.

However, federal laws standardizing LTCI regulations have become outdated and do not include all of the relevant provisions of a specific NAIC Model. For example, neither the HIPAA tax-qualified policies or the Medicaid Partnership Program were ever updated to include the rate stability provisions in the NAIC 2000 Model. These federal laws also do not address recent concerns about the misrepresentation of LTCI by unqualified sales agents nor inappropriate denial of claims. The following section provides more detail about each of these issues.

Premium Instability

Generally, premiums for LTCI are lower when policies are purchased at younger ages. Yet, younger purchasers will also be paying premiums over a longer period of time and long-run stability of premiums is important to ensure their affordability in the future. Although insurers are prohibited from increasing an individual's premium based on a change in the policyholder's circumstances (i.e., increased age or onset of disability), insurers, however, are still able to request permission from a state insurance commissioner to increase premiums for a class of insured.[31]

Comprehensive data on the extent of premium increases across all LTCI companies are not available.

Table 3. Summary of Consumer Protections for LTCI Specified By Different Versions of the NAIC Model Provisions

	1993 NAIC Model Provisions	2000 NAIC Model Provisions	2006 NAIC Model Provisions	2009 NAIC Model Provisions
Revised Pricing and Eligibility for LTCI	Yes	Yes	Yes	Yes
Strengthened Suitability and Rate Stability Provisions	No	Yes	Yes	Yes
Imposed Stricter Criteria for Training and Certification of Insurance Agents	No	No	Yes	Yes
Independent Review of Benefit Trigger Denials	No	No	No	Yes
Current Federal Law Requirements	Health Insurance Portability and Accountability Act (P.L. 104-191)	Deficit Reduction Act of 2005 (P.L. 109-171)[a]	None	None

Source: Congressional Research Service.

Notes: The term NAIC Model Provisions includes both the Model Regulations and the Model Law promulgated by the NAIC.

[a] The LTCI Partnership consumer protections described in the Deficit Reduction Act of 2005 did not include the rate stability language in the NAIC 2000 Model provisions.

However, press reports suggest that major LTCI carriers have applied for or received approval for premium increases between 10% and 40% in one or more states.[32] In addition, the Office of Personnel Management (OPM) announced that premium rates for current federal workers enrolled in the federal LTCI program who had purchased automatic compound inflation protection would increase 25% for most policyholders. These rate increases were a result of a new negotiated LTCI contract for federal workers that included a new benefit option with increased home health care reimbursements, new benefit periods, and higher daily benefit amounts. However, current enrollees who did experience premium increases were provided the opportunity to keep their current premiums substantially the same by making changes to their benefit package.[33]

Premium increases can be necessitated by inadequate medical underwriting, premiums that were initially set too low, or insufficient growth in reserves to cover future claims.[34] Thus, premium or rate stability depends largely on the ability of insurers to adequately predict future claims. In addition, lower than predicted voluntary termination (lapse) rates and lower than predicted rates of return on investments have been cited as a key reason for the most recent round of increases.

Initially, in 2000, the NAIC revised its model provisions to require companies to provide actuarial information to certify the adequacy of all proposed rates and to show that the vast majority of premium increases are devoted to paying claims. In addition, when premiums are increased, 85% of the increased portion of the premium must be available to cover claims. Further, the 2000 NAIC Model Act requires reimbursement of unnecessary rate increases to policyholders. Policyholders are also provided the option to escape the effect of rising rate spirals by being guaranteed the right to switch to another lower premium policy. Finally, the 2000 NAIC Model provisions authorized the commissioner to ban from the market place for five years companies that persist in filing inadequate initial premiums. But most states have not adopted the full NAIC Model language for premium stability.[35]

To address these concerns, the NAIC is currently re-evaluating its rate stability model language. Under the current model regulation an actuarial certification is required when companies submit a premium increase. Specifically, the NAIC model provision states that:

> "The initial premium rate schedule is sufficient to cover anticipated costs under *moderately adverse*_experience and that the premium rate schedule is reasonably expected to be sustainable over the life of the form with no future premium increases anticipated."

The NAIC has recognized that there are potential problems with the "moderately adverse" language because there is no explicit definition of what this means. As a result, the interpretation relies on the judgment of the pricing actuary which makes it difficult to regulate, even for states with an actuary on staff. Regulators are poorly equipped to judge the reasonableness of the company's assumptions.[36] To address these concerns, the NAIC is currently exploring various options to strengthen its rate stability standards including the development of a more concrete definition of "moderately adverse events."

Inappropriate Sales Practices

Following the 1993 NAIC Model Act, there had been a concern that some private sector insurers and agents were inappropriately selling products to persons with low income and assets who may otherwise be eligible for public assistance under Medicaid. In other words, these LTCI policies would not be *suitable* for certain individuals given their circumstances. There was also a concern that individuals may not fully understand the future value of the benefits they purchase. To address these issues, the 2000 NAIC Model required insurers to develop and use suitability standards, and to train agents with respect to the standards. Both insurers and agents must ascertain an applicant's ability to pay and his or her goals and needs through the use of a personal worksheet. There are a number of disclosure requirements related to suitability, including the requirement that the agent and insurer must distribute to the potential policyholder a brochure on the "Things to Know Before You Buy." Since then, the 2006 NAIC Model added provisions concerning training of insurance agents to address concerns about suitability. The 2006 Model also includes a new section on producer (insurance agent) training, which requires producers to complete a one-time eight-hour training course before selling LTCI. According to the NAIC, as of November 2008, 27 states have some form of agent's licensing requirements in their state legislation, but not all of them comply fully with the 2006 NAIC Model Act language.[37]

Inappropriate Denial of Claims

There has been anecdotal evidence that some LTCI policyholders are having difficulty in accessing their benefits once a claim is filed.[38] Recent actions by the NAIC against a large LTCI company have heightened these concerns. National level data from the NAIC have also shown that the number of complaints regarding LTCI has increased between 2004 and 2006.[39] One of the key areas for complaints is the denial of claims. Although the number of claims denials has increased, the increase is not as large when adjusted by the number of claims submitted. The total percentage of claims denied for all policies increased since 2004 from 3.2% to 3.9% in 2006. The percentage of claims denied for comprehensive policies increased from 4.1% to 4.9% over the same period.[40] This data reflects activity from 2004 to 2006 and does not provide any information on more recent years.

Denial of claims can occur for a number of reasons. For example, a number of issues within the reimbursement process could lead to a delay in payment. The first relates to the eligibility for payments from the insurer. The policyholder (or his/her guardian) must notify the insurer and document that the policy has been "triggered." For example, for non-cognitive impairments this means the policyholder meets the requirement of needing assistance with two or more activities of daily living (ADLs).[41] Documentation can include a written statement from the policyholder's physician verifying this information or the insurer may require an assigned care manager to assess eligibility. Thus, a claim can be denied if the insurer does not receive supporting documentation regarding eligibility for payment in a timely manner.

Another reason for denying a claim is that the policyholder has not yet reached the end of the policy's elimination period. Between 2004 and 2006, denied claims for home care only policies because the elimination period had not been met increased 16.3%, for comprehensive policies they increased 37.5%. Finally, denied claims for nursing home benefits where the elimination period had not been met increased 17.7% over the same period.[42]

Although anecdotal evidence raised concerns among policymakers that some insurers are further delaying claims on purpose,[43] national level data from the NAIC do not validate these concerns. According to the NAIC, denial of payments beyond 60 days was not a major issue between 2004 and 2006.[44] Other survey data support the fact that relatively few claims are denied. According to a Lifeplans Survey of 1,500 policyholders over a 21/2-year period, 96% of claims were approved and 4% were denied. Those who conducted the survey suggest this indicates an industry-wide initial claims denial rate of 4%. The same survey reported that the vast majority (93%) of denied claims had a decision rendered within a two-month period and the remaining 7% within another two months.[45]

Although problems in the delay of claims processing are not evident in the NAIC data collected between 2004 and 2006, there is evidence that the problem may be isolated for policies issued by one large insurer. The recent settlement against Conseco, Inc. highlights the use of improper processing practices by the company. In May 2008, state insurance regulators and the NAIC brought a regulatory settlement against Conseco, Inc. for mishandling of LTCI claims. Specifically, claims were not handled in a timely manner and claims files were not documented or maintained. The Conseco investigation found that the primary problem in most cases was a delay in payment of the claim, rather than a denial.

Given these concerns the NAIC adopted in 2009 language to the NAIC Model Act that provides for external independent review of benefit trigger denials. The NAIC also created a subgroup to review existing methods by which companies report claims denials. The subgroup recommended and the NAIC adopted changes to the reporting form so that it is clear which method is being used (per claimant, or per transaction).[46]

Solvency of Long-Term Care Insurance Companies

Following the recent economic downturn, concerns about the long-run solvency of LTCI companies may adversely affect the demand for the product. Amidst this uncertainty, potential LTCI policyholders may decide to wait until the economic situation improves before contemplating a purchase of LTCI. In addition, there are concerns about the guarantee of benefits for current policyholders.

The insurance industry does provide a number of safeguards to protect LTCI policyholders from an insolvent insurer. The current system of protection for LTCI policyholders is called insurance guaranty funds. This interdependent system is a cooperative effort among regulators and insurers in the states where the insolvent insurer operated. It is administered state-by-state and funded by assessments on insurers.[47] When an insurer's financial condition deteriorates to the point where it may have trouble meeting its obligations, it is placed into receivership. In effect, the company and its policies are taken over by the insurance commissioner of the state where the insurer is domiciled. In the absence of bankruptcy, the commissioner may need to establish a plan to ensure policyholders receive coverage or benefits. For example, the insurance commissioner may allow other insurers to purchase parts of the troubled insurer's business. If, however, the company is liquidated, a state guaranty association may need to assume or reinsure policies of the failed insurer.

State law requires insurers to become members of the guaranty associations in each state in which they are licensed to do business. For health and LTCI, the average coverage is about $100,000. One concern about guaranty funds is that the amount of coverage per policy may not be sufficient to insure future potential losses due to insolvency. This does raise the possibility that the guaranty funds would have to raise premium rates and potentially reduce benefits for current policyholders in the future if even a few insurers become insolvent.

Efforts to Expand Participation in the Long-Term Care Insurance Market

If participation rates increase in the private LTCI market, most actuaries agree that the overall costs of policies may be further reduced because the available risk-pool would be larger. Specifically, one of the key premises of insurance is to spread risk across as large a population as possible. Adverse selection occurs when individuals who expect to have a higher risk of needing LTSS in the future (e.g., family history of Alzheimer's) are more likely to purchase a policy than those who do not. In a voluntary program, low participation may limit an insurer's ability to spread risk adequately resulting in adverse selection.

When adverse selection is present in a voluntary system, insurers must charge higher premiums to cover the higher risk of the insured group. Thus, the greater the participation among the general population, the lower the effects of adverse selection.

Many of the concerns about adverse selection were raised when the CLASS Program under the Patient Protection and Affordable Care Act (ACA, P.L. 111-148, as amended) was enacted, which was intended to be a voluntary, federally administered LTCI program.[48] According to the American Academy of Actuaries, design features of the program, such as guaranteed issue (e.g., no pre-existing condition exclusions), and the voluntary nature of the program may lead to those most likely needing the benefit to opt-in and healthy individuals, who may not need the benefit, to opt-out.[49] It was anticipated that adverse selection would likely lead to higher than average premiums and further reduce demand for the CLASS program among young and healthy individuals.

In fact, after examining the actuarial, marketing, and legal issues for a financially solvent program over the next 75 years, HHS sent a letter to Congress, stating that the Administration does not see a viable path forward for implementation of the CLASS program at this time.[50] On January 2, 2013, The American Taxpayers Relief Act of 2012 (P.L. 112-240), among other things, repealed the CLASS program.

Legislative proposals intended to increase the demand for private LTCI policies, and overall participation rates, may include proposals to

- increase tax incentives to lower the after-tax cost of policies,
- improve consumer protections and increase consumer confidence in the product, and
- expand consumer education.

The following describes these proposals in greater detail.

Expand Tax Incentives to Improve Affordability

Under current law, premiums paid by employees may be subject to a premium conversion arrangement under a cafeteria plan (flexible spending type account) and deductible from their taxable income. There are also other tax credits available to certain individuals who purchase health care insurance in the individual market.[51] However, LTCI premiums currently do not have as generous tax incentives as health insurance. But a recent survey by AHIP suggests that increased tax incentives may increase the demand for LTCI. Specifically, according to the AHIP survey, 87% of respondents who chose not to purchase LTCI said they would be "much more interested" or "more interested" if they could deduct premiums from their taxable income.[52]

This section will first discuss the current tax treatment of LTCI and then detail potential legislative proposals and their implications for after-tax LTCI premiums.

Current Tax Treatment

Under current law, there are some tax advantages provided to some aspects of private LTCI. Benefits from a "qualified" LTCI policy are excluded from the gross income of the taxpayer (i.e., they are exempt from taxation).[53] In addition, premiums for LTCI are allowed as itemized deductions to the extent they and other unreimbursed medical expenses exceed 10% of adjusted gross income (AGI) for those under age 65 and 7.5% of AGI for those 65 and older.[54] LTCI premium deductions, however, are subject to age-adjusted limits. In 2013, these limits range annually from $360 for persons aged 40 or younger up to $4,550 for persons over the age of 70.

In addition, under current law, employer contributions toward the cost of tax-qualified LTCI policies are excluded from the gross income of the employee. Self-employed individuals are allowed to include LTCI premiums in calculating their deductions for health insurance expenses. Only amounts less than or equal to the age-adjusted limits can be deducted or excluded from taxable income.

In addition, the Medicare Prescription Drug, Improvement and Modernization Act of 2003 (P.L. 108-173) authorized Health Savings Accounts (HSAs), which allow individuals to pay for LTCI premiums on a tax-advantaged basis. Individuals are eligible to establish and contribute to an HSA if they have a qualifying high deductible health plan (HDHP). Individuals enrolled in Medicare are excluded. Withdrawals from HSAs are exempt from federal income taxes if used for purchase of LTCI.[55]

As noted earlier, a number of legislative changes to the tax code have enabled insurers to develop hybrid products that combine LTCI with either an annuity or a life insurance product. The Pension Protection Act (PPA) of 2006 simplified tax rules regarding combination products (effective in 2010) and added a tax provision specifying that proceeds from an annuity can be used tax-free to purchase a tax-qualified LTCI policy (under Section 7702B(b) of the Internal Revenue Code (IRC)). PPA also allows individuals to use the cash surrender value of a life insurance policy as payment for a tax-qualified LTCI policy and exclude these payments from taxable income. Finally, PPA revised Section 1035 of the IRC to allow for tax-free exchanges of certain insurance contracts. Under this provision, no gain or loss is recognized on the exchange of a life insurance contract, an endowment contract, an annuity contract for a qualified LTCI contract or the exchange of one qualified LTCI contract for another.

Legislative Proposals To Expand Tax Incentives

Expanding tax incentives for long-term care insurance may improve the affordability of policies by reducing the after-tax cost of policies and increasing the demand for LTCI. To do this, LTCI premiums could be included in one or more of the following options:

- an employer-sponsored cafeteria or flexible spending account plan, which would exclude them from gross income;
- as an "above-the-line" tax deduction to arrive at AGI; or
- as a credit against tax liability ("tax credit").

Table 4 summarizes the advantages and disadvantages of each option.

Include in Cafeteria and Flexible Spending Accounts

Cafeteria plans are employer-established benefit plans under which employees may choose between receiving cash (typically additional taxable take-home pay) and certain non-taxable benefits. Under this option, LTCI would be an eligible benefit within the plan and the employee would not be taxed on the value of the benefit. This arrangement reduces both income and employment taxes (i.e., Social Security and Medicare payroll taxes). Under some of the current legislative proposals, LTCI could also be an eligible expense in a flexible spending account (FSA). FSAs and cafeteria plans are closely related, but not all cafeteria plans have FSAs and not all FSAs are part of cafeteria plans.

Table 4. Advantages and Disadvantages to Taxpayers of Alternative Tax Incentives for LTCI Premiums

Tax Treatment of LTC Insurance Premiums	Advantages	Disadvantages
Cafeteria Plan or Flexible Spending Account	Not limited to taxpayers who itemize. Reduces AGI for purposes of other tax provisions. Lowers wage base for Social Security and Medicare taxes on wages.	Only available if the employer offers a cafeteria or flexible spending plan.
Above-the-Line Deduction	Not limited to taxpayers who itemize. Reduces AGI for purposes of other tax provisions.	Required to pay Social Security and Medicare payroll taxes on income used to fund premiums.
Tax Credit	Reduces regular tax liability by amount of credit.	Non-refundable tax credit. If tax liability is less than the credit amount then taxpayer would not benefit from full credit.

Source: Congressional Research Service.

Reimbursements through an FSA are also exempt from income and employment taxes.[56] Including LTCI in a cafeteria plan or FSA would also reduce adjusted gross income for purposes of other tax provisions. Cafeteria plans and FSAs only benefit individuals whose employer has established such plans.[57] For an individual filer with $55,000 in gross income and in the 25% tax bracket, this option would reduce the effective cost of the premiums by 32.65% (this includes a reduction in employment taxes of 7.65% as well).[58]

Above-the-Line Deduction

Under this option, LTCI premiums would be deducted from a taxpayer's gross income. An abovethe-line deduction also reduces adjusted gross income for other tax provisions. The key difference from a cafeteria plan is that the provision is available to everyone and not limited to those employers who offer a plan. In addition, under this option, LTCI premiums (even if deducted from gross income) would still be subject to employment taxes if the individual were employed. For an individual filer with $55,000 in income and in the 25% tax bracket, this option would reduce after-tax LTCI premiums by 25%.

Tax Credit

A tax credit is applied directly against a taxpayer's tax liability. The key distinction in a tax credit is whether it is refundable or nonrefundable. A fully refundable tax credit is paid to the taxpayer even if the amount of the credit exceeds the taxpayer's tax liability. Under a nonrefundable credit, if the tax liability is less than the credit amount of all refundable credits available, then the taxpayer would not benefit from the full credit. Under this option, after tax premiums for the individual filer with $55,000 in gross income would decline dollar for dollar by the amount of the tax credit if the individual's tax liability was equal to or exceeded the amount of all available tax credits.

Other Provisions

Although the discussion above provides a brief overview of the impact of the different options, actual tax savings will vary depending on the specific details of each of the proposals.

To minimize the cost to the federal government, many of the current legislative proposals would not allow the full deduction or credit of premiums initially. Instead these proposals would

- phase-in the deduction or credit over time;
- base the percentage of LTCI premiums that is deductible or creditable on the number of years a policy is held; or
- limit the income from which a deduction can be taken, allowing only a deduction from gross income for distributions from a 401(k) or IRA.

Improve Consumer Protections

As the market for LTCI expands, there is a growing concern that current regulations may not be sufficient to protect consumers from potential abuses in claims administration and processing and future rate stability.

To address these issues, legislative proposals that are introduced to expand tax incentives for LTCI may also require these tax-qualified policies to meet specific NAIC Model Regulations and Laws. (See *Table 3* for a summary of different versions of the NAIC Model provisions with respect to consumer protections.)

Expand Consumer Education

The Long-Term Care Awareness Campaign is a joint federal-state initiative to increase awareness among the American public about the importance of planning for future LTC needs. The Own Your Future Campaign is a collaboration of the Centers for Medicare & Medicaid Services (see http://www.cms.hhs.gov), the Office of the Assistant Secretary for Planning & Evaluation (see http://www.aspe.hhs.gov), and the Administration on Aging (see http://www.aoa.gov), and it has support from the National Governors Association (see http://www.nga.org). The program was started in January 2005. The project's core activities are state-based direct mail campaigns supported by each participating state's governor, and targeted to households with members between the ages of 45 to 70. Campaign materials include a Long-Term Care Planning Kit and state specific information and resources in both print and on the internet. As of January 2010, 25 states have participated in the Long-term Care Campaign to increase awareness of the need to plan for future LTSS.

The response from consumers to the first two phases of the Own Your Future Campaign exceeded expectations, both in terms of consumer interest and in initiating LTSS planning actions. Research following a five-state phase of the campaign indicated that individuals who received the planning kit were twice as likely to take some type of LTSS planning action as compared to those who did not receive the kit. Based on these successes, Congress provided additional support for these education initiatives by establishing the National Clearinghouse for Long-Term Care Information under the Deficit Reduction Act of 2005. Under Section 6021(d) of the act, Congress appropriated $15 million in funding for the National Clearinghouse over five years (2006 to 2010). While ACA had extended funding for the Clearinghouse to 2015 in enacting the CLASS program, the recently enacted American Taxpayers Relief Act of 2012, in repealing the CLASS program, also rescinds the unobligated balance of ACA's funds for the National Clearinghouse.

Legislative proposals in the 113th Congress may expand or extend further into the future funding for the National Clearinghouse.

End Notes

[1] Connie J. Evashwick, "The Continuum of Long-Term Care: An Integrated Systems Approach," 2004.

[2] P. Kemper, H.L. Komisar, and L. Alecxih, "Long-Term Care Over An Uncertain Future: What Can Future Retirees Expect?" Inquiry 42, winter 2005-2006.

[3] CRS Report R42345, Long-Term Services and Supports: Overview and Financing, coordinated by Kirsten J. Colello.

[4] The income and asset criteria vary by state.

[5] See footnote 3.

[6] Genworth Financial, Executive Summary: Genworth 2012 Cost of Care Survey, April 20, 2012.

[7] Ibid.

[8] America's Health Insurance Plans, "Who Buys Long-Term Care Insurance in 2010-2011? A Twenty Year Study of Buyers and Non-Buyers in the Individual Market," March 2012.

[9] U.S. Government Accountability Office, "Long-Term Care Insurance: Federal Program Compared Favorably with Other Products, and Analysis of Claims Trend Could Inform Future Decisions," March 2006.

[10] C. Pfau, D. Helwig and A. Schmitz, "2011Individual Long-Term Care Insurance Survey," Broker World Magazine, July 2011.

[11] U.S. Government Accountability Office, "Long-Term Care Insurance: Federal Program Compared Favorably with Other Products, and Analysis of Claims Trend Could Inform Future Decisions," March 2006.

[12] These provisions are also specified in the Social Security Act Title XIX Section 1917(b)(5)(42 U.S.C. 1396p(b)(5)).

[13] The Social Security Act requires states to recover from a beneficiary's estate certain amounts Medicaid paid for LTSS and other services.

[14] Most Medicaid applicants may protect no more than $2,000 in assets for an individual and $3,000 for a married couple. In general, Partnership Program policy owners may protect amounts equivalent to the value of the benefits paid by the LTCI policy purchased (e.g., $100,000 of nursing home or assisted living benefits paid enables that individual to retain up to $100,000 in assets and still qualify for Medicaid coverage in that state). This is referred to as the dollar-fordollar model. Two states have exceptions to this design model. New York uses a total asset protection model in which purchasers with certain state-approved policies may qualify for Medicaid while retaining all of their assets. Indiana uses a hybrid model, offering both dollar-for-dollar and total asset protection.

[15] Iowa received approval from the Secretary of HHS to operate a program before OBRA 93, but it did not fully do so.

[16] The DRA also added new minimum federal requirements for LTCI plans to qualify as Partnership policies. Among these requirements are consumer protections related to inflation protection, unintentional lapse, disclosure, and nonforfeiture of benefits.

[17] Thomson Reuters, The Long-Term Care Partnership Program: 5 Years After Enactment Under the Deficit Reduction Act, October 17, 2011.

[18] The states that have not yet adopted a DRA Partnership Program are AK, DE, HI, IL, MA, MI, MS, NM, UT, and VT as indicated on http://w2.dehpg.net/LTCPartnership/ State Reciprocity.aspx as of January 15, 2013.

[19] Thomson Reuters, The Long-Term Care Partnership Program: 5 Years After Enactment Under the Deficit Reduction Act, October 17, 2011.

[20] J. Douglas and K. Fisherkeller, "U.S. Individual Long-Term Care Insurance: 2011 Supplement," LIMRA, 2011.

[21] R. Johnson and J. Park, "Who Purchases Long-Term Care Insurance," Urban Institute, Issue Brief, No. 29, March 2011.

[22] Once the policy is purchased, premiums cannot increase with age, but they can increase for other reasons.

[23] America's Health Insurance Plans, "Who Buys Long-Term Care Insurance in 2010-2011? A Twenty Year Study of Buyers and Non-Buyers in the Individual Market," March 2012.

[24] Medicare covers up to 100 days of post-hospital care for skilled nursing or rehabilitative services on a daily basis (after a three-day hospital stay). There is no beneficiary cost-sharing for the first 20 days. Days 21-100 are subject to daily coinsurance charges ($144.50 in 2012).

[25] Medicare covers visits by personnel from a participating home health agency for beneficiaries who, among other requirements, (1) are confined to home, (2) need skilled nursing care on an intermittent basis, or (3) need physical or occupational therapy or speech language therapy. The services must be provided under a plan of care established by a physician for a 60-day episode of care.

[26] America's Health Insurance Plans, "Who Buys Long-Term Care Insurance in 2010-2011? A Twenty Year Study of Buyers and Non-Buyers in the Individual Market," March 2012.

[27] America's Health Insurance Plans, "Who Buys Long-Term Care Insurance in 2010-2011? A Twenty Year Study of Buyers and Non-Buyers in the Individual Market," March 2012.

[28] Kemper et al., "Long Term Care Over An Uncertain Future: What Can Current Retirees Expect," Inquiry, winter 2005-2006.

[29] NAIC's Compendium of State Laws on Insurance Topics, Long-Term Care Insurance Act Provisions, November 2011.

[30] These provisions for tax-qualification are also specified in the Internal Revenue Code (IRC) Section 7702(B)).

[31] A class of insured is generally defined as all individuals of the same age with the same policy in the same state and with the same coverage.

[32] A. Tergesen and L. Scism, "Long-Term Premiums Soar," Wall Street Journal, October 16, 2010.

[33] Office of Personnel Management, "OPM Awards New Long Term Care Insurance Contract," press release, May 1, 2009.

[34] R. Desonia, "The Promise and Reality of Long-Term Care Insurance," National Health Policy Forum. 2004.

[35] NAIC's Compendium of State Laws on Insurance Topics, Long-Term Care Insurance Act Provisions, February 2009.

[36] T. Serbinowksi, Utah Insurance Department, Presentation at the 12th Annual Intercompany Long-Term Care Insurance Conference, "Academy Practice Note Revisions and NAIC Model Regulation: Issues Relating to Rate Stability," March 20, 2012.

[37] NAIC's Compendium of State Laws on Insurance Topics, Long-Term Care Insurance Act Provisions, February 2009.

[38] U.S. Congress, House Committee on Energy and Commerce, Subcommittee on Oversight and Investigation, Long-Term Care Insurance: Are Consumers Protected for the Long-Term?, hearing, July 24, 2008.

[39] National Association of Insurance Commissioners, "Long-Term Care Data Call and Analysis Report," May 9, 2008.

[40] National Association of Insurance Commissioners, "Long-Term Care Data Call and Analysis Report," May 9, 2008.

[41] ADLs include eating, bathing, dressing, toileting, transferring, or walking across the room.

[42] National Association of Insurance Commissioners, "Long-Term Care Data Call and Analysis Report," May 9, 2008.

[43] Charles Duhigg, "Aged, Frail and Denied Care by Their Insurers," New York Times, March 26, 2007.

[44] National Association of Insurance Commissioners, "Long-Term Care Data Call and Analysis Report," May 9, 2008.

[45] Testimony of M. Cohen, president, LifePlans, Inc., before the U.S. House Committee on Energy and Commerce, Subcommittee on Oversight and Investigation, Long-Term Care Insurance: Are Consumers Protected for the Long-Term?, hearings, July 24, 2008.

[46] Based on conversations with NAIC staff on April 21, 2009.

[47] For more information on these funds, see CRS Report RL32175, Insurance Guaranty Funds, by Baird Webel.

[48] For a complete description of the CLASS program provisions, see CRS Report R40842, Community Living Assistance Services and Supports (CLASS) Provisions in the Patient Protection and Affordable Care Act (ACA), by Janemarie Mulvey and Kirsten J. Colello.

[49] Ibid.

[50] Letter from Kathleen G. Sebelius, Secretary of Health and Human Services, to Representative John Boehner, Speaker of the House, October 14, 2011, http://www.hhs.gov/secretary/letter 10142011.html.

[51] See CRS Report RL32620, Health Coverage Tax Credit, by Bernadette Fernandez.

[52] America's Health Insurance Plans, "Who Buys Long-Term Care Insurance in 2010-2011? A Twenty Year Study of Buyers and Non-Buyers in the Individual Market," March 2012.

[53] Health Insurance Portability and Accountability Act, P.L. 104-191 and Section 7702B(b) of the Internal Revenue Code.

[54] This percentage will increase from 7.5% to 10% in 2016 for those age 65 and older due to changes in IRC 213(d) enacted by ACA.

[55] CRS Report RL33257, Health Savings Accounts: Overview of Rules for 2012, by Janemarie Mulvey.

[56] See CRS Report RL33505, Tax Benefits for Health Insurance and Expenses: Overview of Current Law, by Janemarie Mulvey.

[57] Retired workers are not likely to have coverage, as they would not have access to a cafeteria plan and only a former employer and not the individual covered contributes to a retiree's FSA.

[58] Example assumes a 50-year old individual who is a single tax filer with no dependents, earns $55,000 a year and is in the 25% tax bracket.

INDEX

A

accommodation, 12
accountability, 13, 78, 92, 99, 103
accounting, 7, 64, 131
accreditation, 31, 38
ACL, 36, 37, 41
ADA, 81, 83, 87
adjustment, 37, 39, 75
administrative support, 89, 90
administrators, 15
adults, 6, 7, 10, 12, 14, 15, 18, 19, 20, 21, 23, 24, 26, 35, 37, 44, 58, 59, 105, 118, 119, 120
advancement, 17, 40, 46
adverse event, 139
age, viii, 6, 7, 9, 10, 18, 20, 21, 22, 23, 24, 54, 56, 58, 66, 70, 80, 81, 83, 86, 118, 124, 125, 127, 131, 132, 137, 144, 150, 151
agencies, 4, 11, 15, 17, 28, 30, 31, 35, 40, 46, 48, 86, 95, 98, 101, 107
aging population, 40
Alaska, 136
Americans with Disabilities Act, 81
annual rate, 135
anxiety, 42
appropriations, 107
arthritis, 7
assessment, 11, 14, 30, 34, 35, 37, 41, 42, 67, 83, 90, 95, 99, 103, 104, 105, 106
assessment tools, 34, 95, 103
asset development, 71
assets, 18, 20, 21, 22, 23, 24, 50, 53, 54, 59, 61, 72, 74, 82, 83, 84, 119, 122, 140, 149
assistive technology, 18, 57, 58, 71, 72, 83
attachment, 16
attitudes, 81, 121
audit(s), 101, 102
authority(s), 12, 80, 86, 87, 88, 92, 98
autonomy, 87
average costs, 68
awareness, 37, 41, 43, 54, 148

B

baby boomers, vii, 50, 125, 126
ban, 139
bankruptcy, 142
barriers, 43, 46, 53, 61, 78, 103
base, 103, 122, 146, 147
behaviors, 62, 94
benchmarks, 87
beneficiaries, 8, 14, 23, 31, 39, 61, 78, 85, 86, 88, 89, 92, 93, 94, 100, 120, 150
benefits, 7, 17, 18, 22, 23, 26, 31, 40, 48, 50, 53, 56, 57, 58, 66, 68, 69, 71, 74, 75, 82, 99, 108, 118, 127, 130, 135, 136, 137, 140, 141, 142, 145, 149

bias, 85, 88, 89
birth rate, 10
blood, 43
blood pressure, 43
bottom-up, 99
brain, 43
building blocks, 102
Bureau of Labor Statistics, 48
burnout, 44
businesses, 9, 70
buyer(s), 122, 131, 132

C

campaigns, 52, 70, 72, 133, 148
candidates, 122
care model, 47, 94
career development, 109
caregivers, vii, 2, 4, 6, 9, 10, 11, 12, 18, 27, 28, 29, 30, 32, 33, 35, 36, 37, 39, 40, 41, 42, 43, 44, 45, 50, 63, 67, 85, 86, 88, 91, 92, 95, 99, 105, 106, 107, 109, 118, 119, 124, 133
caregiving, 4, 9, 10, 27, 39, 43, 44, 70, 105, 106, 107, 119
cash, 57, 66, 145
CBS, 12, 29, 86, 100
Census, 3, 7, 118
certification, 17, 31, 38, 48, 49, 55, 108, 139
challenges, 4, 5, 11, 14, 28, 76
charitable organizations, 33
Chicago, 112, 116, 119
children, 10, 55, 61, 70
chronic illness, 9
citizens, 101
civil rights, 81
clarity, 50, 73
cleaning, 5
clients, 85, 93, 94, 96, 108
climate, 89
closure, 104
cognitive impairment, viii, 50, 63, 64, 125, 127, 140
collaboration, 102, 148
commercial, 33
communication, 42, 43, 103
community service, 92
community-based services, 8, 12, 16, 29, 31, 37, 70, 78, 86, 87, 94, 98, 99, 100, 108
comorbidity, 7
compensation, 17, 46, 69
competition, 57, 66, 72
complexity, viii, 10, 30, 79, 126, 127, 131, 132, 133, 135, 136
compliance, 123, 136
complications, 93
composition, 129
conference, 110
confinement, 130
congress, v, vii, viii, 1, 30, 41, 46, 51, 58, 59, 62, 80, 102, 110, 112, 122, 125, 126, 143, 148, 150
Congressional Budget Office, 26, 88, 118, 123
consensus, 62, 91, 110
consolidation, 130
constituents, 64
consumer choice, 28, 85
consumer education, viii, 126, 127, 143
consumer protection, viii, 45, 57, 69, 74, 85, 93, 126, 127, 131, 132, 136, 137, 138, 143, 147, 149
consumers, 14, 17, 22, 31, 33, 35, 36, 37, 38, 45, 47, 53, 57, 63, 66, 69, 73, 74, 84, 85, 91, 101, 147, 148
conversations, 151
cooperation, 35, 72
coordination, 4, 6, 12, 27, 28, 32, 33, 34, 56, 64, 79, 91, 92, 93, 94, 96, 98, 102, 103, 106, 107
cost effectiveness, 44
cost saving, 44, 97
counseling, 14, 35, 100, 101
covering, 66
CPI, 100, 133, 134
credentials, 46
crowds, 22
cultural tradition, 41
curriculum, 46, 49

D

daily living, vii, 1, 5, 12, 55, 79, 118, 127, 140
data collection, 48, 91
deduction, 146, 147
deficiencies, 9, 17, 104
delegates, 110
dementia, 7, 10, 107, 109
democracy, 98
demographic data, 131
demonstrations, 14, 38, 46
denial, 81, 137, 140, 141
Department of Health and Human Services, 41, 102, 110, 122
Department of Justice, 46
depression, 10
depth, 62
detection, 43
diabetes, 7
dignity, vii, 2, 12
direct mail, 148
directors, 97
disability, 9, 14, 18, 19, 21, 39, 50, 52, 57, 58, 66, 70, 71, 73, 76, 83, 86, 87, 96, 118, 123, 124, 127, 137
disclosure, 140, 149
distribution, 19, 53, 74, 122
diversity, 99
draft, 110

E

earnings, 23, 50, 81, 82, 83
Easter, 112
economic downturn, 142
economic growth, 67
economic status, 9
education, 4, 25, 43, 61, 71, 107, 108, 110, 148
elderly population, 18, 119
eligibility criteria, 14
emergency, 82, 95, 102
emergency response, 95
emotional health, 64
employees, 9, 40, 55, 70, 76, 107, 131, 144, 145
employers, 55, 70, 73, 106, 107, 129, 146
employment, 7, 15, 18, 33, 45, 58, 59, 61, 71, 80, 83, 96, 109, 145, 146
employment opportunities, 59
enrollment, 13, 29, 87, 88, 89
environment(s), viii, 12, 63, 74, 93, 126, 132
equipment, 107, 133
equity, 54, 84, 102
evidence, 32, 41, 42, 44, 68, 77, 85, 106, 140, 141
evidence-based practices, 106
evidence-based program, 85
evolution, 81
exclusion, 68
execution, 99, 111
exercise, 50
expenditures, 19, 24, 25, 28, 29, 69, 100, 122

F

FAA, 111
families, 2, 4, 5, 6, 8, 10, 11, 12, 18, 20, 21, 23, 27, 28, 30, 35, 36, 40, 51, 54, 61, 62, 63, 64, 69, 70, 71, 73, 85, 86, 89, 101, 106, 107, 120, 121, 123, 131
family history, 143
family members, 6, 10, 14, 64, 105, 119, 124
family support, 13
FBI, 45
FDA, 72
federal agency, 47
federal government, 45, 75, 83, 84, 92, 99, 100, 104, 107, 114, 128, 129, 137, 147
federal law, 59, 104, 137
federal regulations, 70, 73
Federal Reserve, 54, 74, 116
financial, viii, 2, 4, 9, 10, 11, 13, 20, 21, 22, 28, 39, 49, 50, 51, 52, 54, 57, 64, 68, 69,

70, 71, 76, 84, 94, 98, 105, 107, 108, 125, 126, 136, 142
financial condition, 142
financial incentives, 13, 84, 94
financial performance, 22
financial planning, 52, 68, 69
financial resources, viii, 4, 11, 21, 49, 51, 125, 126
financial stability, 64, 136
financial support, 9
flaws, 80
flexibility, 26, 45, 52, 53, 85, 89, 100
force, 22, 105, 110, 129, 131
formation, 75
formula, 56, 65
functional impairments, vii, 2, 6, 10, 18, 21, 27, 90, 92
funding, 11, 12, 13, 18, 20, 27, 28, 31, 34, 36, 44, 52, 54, 56, 59, 70, 71, 76, 96, 98, 121, 128, 148
funds, 27, 34, 54, 61, 69, 70, 71, 73, 93, 96, 97, 104, 107, 122, 128, 142, 148, 151

G

GAO, 24, 64, 122
GDP, 100
Georgia, 94
Georgians, 95
glucose, 43
GNP, 26, 111, 123
government expenditure, 68
governments, 3, 28, 136
governor, 148
grass, 98
grassroots, 33
Great Recession, 74
growth, 17, 25, 26, 87, 100, 129, 131, 133, 135, 138
growth rate, 26
guardian, 77, 114, 140
guidance, 72
guidelines, 136

H

Hawaii, 98
Health and Human Services, 110, 119, 151
health care, 4, 6, 9, 11, 13, 28, 29, 31, 32, 33, 34, 40, 43, 46, 47, 52, 54, 56, 61, 62, 70, 71, 75, 76, 82, 83, 86, 89, 91, 94, 95, 107, 108, 128, 131, 136, 138, 144
health care costs, 4
health care programs, 54
health care system, 31, 32, 89
health condition, 5, 6, 39, 94, 99
health expenditure, 94
health information, 43, 107
health insurance, 22, 50, 58, 75, 76, 80, 82, 83, 108, 123, 129, 144
health services, 14, 60, 94, 121, 133
health status, 47
HHS, 41, 42, 43, 64, 72, 73, 98, 100, 108, 110, 143, 149
higher education, 61
high-risk populations, 94
hiring, 88
Hispanics, 8
historical data, 134
history, 110
home care services, 37, 133
home value, 54
homes, 6, 9, 15, 16, 37, 48, 54, 61, 84, 87, 97, 99, 108
hospice, 55
hospitalization, 11, 36, 59, 60, 89, 90, 93, 97, 106, 128
host, 37
hourly wage, 48, 108
House, vii, 1, 47, 110, 114, 115, 150, 151
House of Representatives, vii, 1, 110, 114
housing, 21, 28, 33, 61, 71, 85, 91, 96, 97, 107, 110
HUD, 96
human, 5, 63
hybrid, 71, 76, 130, 137, 145, 149

I

ID, 124
identification, 97
impairments, vii, 2, 6, 10, 18, 21, 27, 90, 92, 135
improvements, 64, 67, 69
in transition, 92, 93
incidence, 21
income, 7, 18, 20, 21, 23, 29, 50, 53, 54, 56, 57, 58, 59, 65, 68, 70, 76, 77, 78, 80, 81, 82, 83, 84, 86, 87, 92, 96, 97, 98, 99, 101, 108, 118, 122, 124, 128, 140, 144, 145, 146, 147, 149
income support, 7
income tax, 57, 66, 144
independence, vii, 2, 12, 33, 55, 79, 91, 96, 127
independent living, 97
indexing, 84
industry, viii, 16, 126, 127, 130, 141, 142
infancy, 6
inflation, 67, 74, 75, 84, 100, 132, 133, 134, 137, 138, 149
information technology, 37, 95
infrastructure, 90, 98, 100
injections, 45
injury(s), 12, 32, 40, 101, 105
institutions, 8, 15, 97
insurance policy, 53, 75, 130, 145
integration, 5, 31, 40, 43, 81, 87, 91, 93, 103
intellectual disabilities, 6, 38, 123, 124
interest rates, 22, 53, 74, 130
intermediaries, 15
intervention, 41
investment(s), 50, 53, 54, 69, 72, 74, 130, 132, 139
Iowa, 149
IRC, 61, 73, 145, 150, 151
isolation, 105
issues, vii, viii, 20, 21, 30, 55, 59, 62, 63, 79, 104, 109, 110, 126, 132, 136, 137, 140, 147
itemized deductions, 144

J

job satisfaction, 17, 40, 45
jurisdiction, 136

L

labor force, 58
labor market, 59
labor shortage, 108
later life, 118
lattices, 40, 46, 47
laws, viii, 87, 98, 104, 126, 132, 136, 137
laws and regulations, viii, 126, 132, 136
lead, 16, 69, 94, 140, 143
legal issues, 143
legislation, 60, 67, 81, 102, 110, 140
legislative proposals, 144, 145, 147
life expectancy, 19
life-insurance, viii, 126, 129
lifetime, 6, 19, 23, 24, 51, 66, 68, 70, 123, 135
light, 63
litigation, 8
livable communities, 33, 34, 91
living environment, 11
local community, 91
long term care, vii
long-term care insurance, viii, 18, 20, 22, 23, 27, 50, 51, 52, 53, 55, 57, 66, 68, 69, 70, 72, 73, 74, 75, 76, 77, 80, 81, 122, 125, 145
long-term services, vii, 1, 2, 5, 22, 24, 27, 38, 49, 59, 62, 70, 80, 82, 92, 99, 100, 105, 106, 110, 126
long-term services and supports (LTSS), vii, 1, 2, 5, 22, 24, 27, 38, 49, 59, 62, 70, 80, 82, 92, 99, 100, 105, 106, 110, 126
love, 2
LTC, 50, 53, 66, 71, 72, 73, 75, 76, 90, 112, 114, 120, 146, 148

M

macroeconomic environment, 74, 75
magnitude, 48, 49, 62, 128
majority, vii, viii, 1, 6, 9, 15, 39, 41, 86, 101, 125, 126, 139, 141
management, 5, 14, 29, 42, 43, 47, 56, 79, 88, 92, 93, 94, 95, 96, 98, 108, 120
market incentives, 52
market penetration, 50
marketing, 70, 130, 143
materials, 148
matter, 35
MBI, 80, 81, 82, 124
measurement, 37, 38
media, 118
median, 121
medical, 10, 11, 12, 22, 23, 24, 28, 29, 30, 31, 40, 41, 42, 43, 50, 58, 60, 61, 92, 94, 98, 99, 105, 107, 127, 130, 133, 138, 144
medical care, 10, 11, 30, 31, 42, 94, 98, 105
medication, 5, 15, 42, 47
mental health, 6, 55, 79, 97, 123
mental impairment, 34
mentoring, 109
methodology, 104
middle class, 68, 70, 84
minorities, 118
models, 14, 31, 32, 33, 36, 38, 39, 57, 63, 74, 78, 85, 91, 92, 93, 98, 110
modifications, 11, 13
Moon, 89, 116
MSW, 112

N

National Council on Disability, 64, 114
national strategy, 41, 106, 107
needy, 54, 84, 87
nervous system, 6
neutral, 38, 77, 93, 97, 102
New England, 119
New Freedom Initiative, 12
nurses, 15, 45, 99, 109
nursing, 8, 10, 11, 14, 15, 16, 17, 21, 24, 29, 36, 37, 41, 42, 45, 46, 48, 56, 59, 60, 78, 79, 84, 85, 87, 89, 90, 93, 94, 96, 97, 101, 104, 105, 106, 107, 108, 118, 121, 122, 128, 130, 131, 133, 134, 141, 149, 150
nursing care, 59, 60, 89, 101, 150
nursing home, 8, 11, 14, 15, 16, 17, 21, 24, 29, 37, 45, 46, 48, 59, 84, 85, 87, 90, 93, 94, 96, 97, 106, 108, 118, 121, 122, 128, 130, 131, 133, 134, 141, 149

O

Obama, 12
Obama Administration, 12
occupational therapy, 150
Office of Management and Budget, 64
officials, 63
old age, 18
operations, 104
opportunities, 17, 44, 46, 51, 59, 69, 80, 81, 82, 83, 87, 106, 109
outpatient, 56
oversight, 37, 85, 136

P

paralysis, 6
parents, 86, 123
parity, 108
participants, 55, 88
pathways, 17, 81
patient care, 15, 93, 94, 103
payroll, 15, 56, 71, 79, 145, 146
PCA, 120
permission, 33, 137
permit, 44, 45, 95, 97, 109
personal assistance, vii, 2, 7, 16, 18, 57, 58
personal goals, 106
personal responsibility, 65
persons with disabilities, 12, 20, 44, 51, 96, 97
physicians, 15, 90, 99

platform, 32
policy, viii, 8, 22, 36, 40, 51, 53, 54, 67, 77, 92, 94, 97, 110, 119, 123, 125, 126, 127, 129, 130, 131, 132, 133, 134, 135, 136, 139, 140, 141, 142, 143, 144, 145, 147, 149, 150
policy options, 132
policymakers, 75, 141
pools, 73
population, viii, 4, 6, 7, 8, 14, 15, 16, 18, 22, 23, 26, 28, 31, 40, 50, 63, 65, 67, 68, 70, 86, 88, 93, 109, 122, 126, 131, 135, 143
portability, 54, 75
poverty, 58, 122
preparation, 5, 51
present value, 53, 68
preservation, 67
president, vii, 1, 111, 112, 113, 114, 151
prevention, 67, 94, 96
principles, 40
private sector, 139
producers, 140
product design, 22, 53
professionals, 15, 28, 40, 41, 42, 94, 99, 106
profit, 33, 97
project, 34, 57, 58, 97, 148
protection, viii, 51, 52, 53, 54, 65, 66, 77, 125, 127, 132, 133, 134, 137, 138, 142, 149
psychiatrist, 15
psychoactive drug, 17
public assistance, 140
public awareness, 70, 110, 133
public expenditures, 75, 101
public financing, 55
public health, 4
public housing, 96
public policy, 51, 65, 69, 74
public resources, 33, 50, 53, 62, 84
public safety, 52, 57, 65, 77, 98
public sector, 106
public support, 51, 77
public-private partnerships, 53

Q

qualifications, 69
quality of life, 29, 32, 62, 91
quality of living, vii, 2
quality of service, 15
quality standards, 89, 92

R

rating scale, 104
real estate, 84
real time, 95
recession, 25
recognition, 96
recommendations, 2, 62, 63, 67, 88, 89, 106, 110
recovery, 54, 84, 122, 123, 131
recruiting, 109
reform, 88, 92, 94, 110
reform(s), 32, 38, 75, 88, 94, 100, 102, 103, 123
registries, 45, 48, 98
regulations, viii, 35, 57, 71, 72, 73, 78, 85, 101, 126, 130, 136, 137, 147
regulatory agencies, 104
regulatory framework, 75
regulatory requirements, 22
rehabilitation, 22, 39, 60, 109
reimburse, 90
reinsurance, 53, 66, 73
relatives, 106
relaxation, 53, 74
rent, 96, 97
requirements, 17, 20, 30, 32, 45, 54, 71, 73, 74, 80, 88, 90, 93, 108, 120, 122, 124, 130, 136, 137, 140, 149, 150
research funding, 104
researchers, 44, 135
resentment, 68
reserves, 139
Residential, 87, 96
resources, 2, 4, 5, 9, 18, 20, 21, 23, 32, 37, 38, 44, 49, 50, 51, 54, 55, 56, 64, 65, 69,

70, 77, 80, 81, 82, 84, 85, 91, 93, 94, 99, 105, 106, 110, 148
response, 8, 26, 148
restrictions, 104
restructuring, 51
retention rate, 16
retirement, vii, 4, 20, 21, 50, 52, 53, 54, 56, 57, 65, 68, 70, 71, 72, 73, 74, 75, 76, 77, 81, 82, 84, 118, 122, 123, 125, 126, 129, 131
retirement age, 56, 57, 65
retirement annuities, viii, 126
retirement security, viii, 125, 126
rewards, 84
rights, 57
risk(s), viii, 5, 10, 12, 18, 23, 24, 36, 39, 49, 50, 51, 52, 54, 55, 56, 57, 59, 65, 66, 67, 69, 72, 73, 74, 78, 101, 105, 118, 122, 125, 126, 127, 129, 131, 135, 143
risk assessment, 36
risk management, 66, 73
roots, 98
rules, 11, 22, 24, 28, 29, 31, 35, 50, 59, 68, 74, 82, 83, 87, 94, 101, 103, 122, 123, 130, 145

S

safety, 2, 4, 5, 50, 51, 52, 53, 64, 65, 66, 67, 76, 84, 89, 128
savings, vii, 2, 4, 5, 20, 21, 23, 30, 38, 50, 51, 52, 53, 55, 57, 61, 66, 69, 70, 71, 72, 76, 77, 78, 88, 92, 97, 100, 105, 106, 123, 125, 126, 147
savings account, 61, 71, 76
savings rate, 4, 69
scope, 32, 41, 44, 109, 110
secondary education, 25
security, viii, 81, 107, 118, 123, 125, 126
segregation, 118
Senate, vii, 1, 110, 115, 116, 117
service provider, 11
sex, 45
shortage, 16, 44
sibling, 41
signs, 15
Social Security, 22, 23, 53, 56, 58, 64, 65, 68, 72, 79, 81, 83, 114, 117, 145, 146, 149
Social Security Administration, 64
Social Security Disability Insurance, 22, 23, 79
social services, 28
social support, 15
social workers, 15
society, 76, 81
software, 69
solution, 52, 54, 75, 76, 77, 82, 89, 95, 99, 110
speech, 94, 150
spending, viii, 9, 12, 19, 21, 23, 24, 25, 26, 38, 50, 67, 72, 77, 86, 89, 92, 100, 101, 106, 123, 125, 128, 144, 145, 146
SSA, 83
SSI, 58, 82, 86, 95, 103, 122
stability, 79, 132, 137, 138, 139, 147
staffing, 108
stakeholders, 45, 62
standard of living, viii, 50, 125, 126
standardization, 69
state laws, 75
state oversight, 136
state regulators, viii, 126
statutes, 85
stress, 10, 11, 12, 39, 42, 63, 94, 105
strictures, 88
stroke, 7
structure, 5, 46, 51, 52, 54, 55, 63, 82, 96, 102, 105
structuring, 54
style, 17
subsidy(s), 53, 68, 70, 78, 97
supervision, 5, 17, 45, 109
suppliers, 42
support services, 43, 95, 127
Supreme Court, 12, 81
symptoms, 43

T

target, 87, 92, 94
Task Force, 110
tax credits, 123, 144
tax deduction, 73, 145
tax incentive, viii, 75, 126, 131, 143, 144, 145, 147
taxation, 144
taxes, 15, 145, 146
taxpayers, 28, 50, 63, 146
team members, 42
teams, 33, 40, 42, 47, 106, 107, 109
technical assistance, 30, 34
techniques, 105
technology(s), 5, 13, 28, 32, 33, 37, 43, 61, 62, 63, 72, 84, 89, 91
telephone, 130
tenure, 16
terminal illness, 130
testing, 38, 130
therapy, 60, 79, 89, 94, 150
time frame, 38
time periods, 54, 87
top-down, 75, 99
training, 10, 17, 35, 40, 41, 42, 43, 44, 45, 46, 47, 48, 49, 63, 106, 107, 108, 109, 120, 140
training programs, 46, 47
transformation, 91
transportation, 28, 33, 60, 61, 71, 91, 98, 107
Treasury, 64
treatment, 59, 61, 71, 76, 77, 144
tuition, 71
turnover, 16, 17, 40, 48, 108, 121

U

U.S. Treasury, 116
underwriting, 22, 23, 50, 53, 74, 138
uniform, 34, 35, 59, 67, 75, 87, 88, 103
uninsured, 26, 55
United, vii, 1, 14, 15, 81, 86, 105, 111, 112, 114, 118, 119, 121, 123
United States, vii, 1, 14, 15, 81, 86, 105, 114, 118, 121, 123
updating, 69, 78, 108
Urban Institute, 13, 116, 149

V

vacancies, 96, 108
variations, 13
vehicles, 70
vein, 93
Vice President, 111, 112, 113, 115
vision, 51, 83
vote, 1, 2
vouchers, 97

W

wages, 40, 48, 108, 109, 146
waiver, 12, 30, 83, 97, 99, 100
walking, 150
Washington, 14, 31, 75, 93, 100, 118, 120, 122
waste, 94
wealth, 20, 97, 121
wealth distribution, 121
web, 34
well-being, 5, 33
well-being outcomes, 5
wellness, 33, 90
White House, 64, 110
withdrawal, 73
witnesses, 2, 70, 89, 93
workers, 15, 16, 17, 39, 40, 44, 45, 46, 47, 48, 49, 50, 57, 58, 59, 80, 81, 98, 108, 109, 118, 138, 151
workforce, 5, 15, 16, 17, 39, 40, 44, 45, 47, 48, 49, 58, 64, 67, 98, 107, 108, 109, 110
working conditions, 107
workplace, 5, 7, 69, 107
worry, 21